We Who Worship

Workbook

by

Cheryl Salem

We Who Worship Workbook

Seventh Printing

Printed in United States of America

Copyright © 2015 by Salem Family Ministries

ISBN 1-890370-29-0

Salem Family Ministries
PO Box 1595
Cathedral City, CA 92345
www.salemfamilyministries.org

Disclaimer: The views expressed in this workbook contain my personal opinions and experiences throughout my life and time spent in God's presence. I express them as my opinion and view only, and share them with you from my personal lifelong experience from my heart. I am only communicating what has worked for me personally, and what I have personally experienced with the Lord.

We Who Worship Workbook

How to use this workbook

This We Who Worship Workbook is designed to be a companion prayer journal workbook to go with the We Who Worship book. As you read the chapters in We Who Worship take the time to work the pages before the Lord in prayer and time spent with Him, searching your heart, mind, soul, and spirit to develop the highest level of worshiper the Lord has designed you to be. Within the very DNA of your cellular level you were created to worship Him! Like all things human, and on the earth, we must develop what we have been given. Use this time with your Father in the secret place of His presence to bring to the forefront of your personal worship the truth and spirit of who you are designed to be inside your Father God!

Don't hurry. Take your time. This is not a race or even a destiny. This is a journey . . . a journey of His presence to develop the core of your reason for 'being'. He will never leave you nor forsake you. Enjoy each day, each prayer, each moment in His presence as you develop the worshiper within.

Be honest with yourself and your Lord. He deserves it and so do you. Don't 'try', just 'be'. Be still and know that I AM God! This is a promise from heaven for all of us. When you come away in the secret place of His presence you will find who you really are, and what your purpose is.

Relax. Enjoy the ride of His Spirit. You are a worshiper. You don't 'do' worship. You 'are' worship. So just be who you were created to be.

School of Worship

Purpose:

To raise up worshipers with a clean heart, called to be instruments of worship by the Holy Spirit. To define the innate difference between worshiper and musician, singer, dancer, artist, performer, etc. This School of Worship is for those who are willing to lay down their lives, to be completely His, to live and to be used by Him with humility, purity, integrity, and accountability.

This is a school of heart first, then of thought and purpose. I ask you to seek the Lord over these coming days, listen, write down what He tells you, and obey His voice. Ask the Lord to show you what He longs for you to know. Ask the Father to reveal to you His specific purpose, for you, in this great scheme of your life of worship. Ask yourself:

Where do I fit as a worshiper?

_____
_____
_____

What am I already doing right?

_____
_____
_____

What do I need to change to come even closer to His throne and bow down before Him?

_____
_____
_____

Worship is about the journey, the romance, with the Lord. Your concern here is not about the destination but the daily pursuit of the Lover of your soul from this day all the way into eternity. This 'road of worship' is not a sprint but rather a marathon, so pace yourself in His presence to be able to go the distance.

Worship is about the rhythm of our romance with the One who gave Himself for us. Song of Solomon 6:3, "I am my beloved's and my beloved is mine."

I may be familiar to you because we have met many times before as worshipers. Come with me today and we will worship the King together. Look for me! I will meet you at His feet! Oh, that's where I know you! I have been with you at His feet many times before but not nearly as many as we will experience into eternity! Come up higher, and I will show you . . . YOURSELF, as His highest worshiper!

Chapter One
The Heart of a Worshiper

John 4:23-24

"But the hour is coming, and now is, when the true worshipers will worship the Father in spirit and truth; for the Father is seeking such to worship Him. God is spirit, and those who worship Him must worship in spirit and truth."

We have had a generation of worshipers who are 'doing' worship, but God has called us in these last days to rebuild worship and take it back to the very 'being' of a worshiper. We must become what we were created to become. Worship is in our 'being'. Worship is in our DNA; it is who we were sent to the earth to develop into, this reverberating frequency of pure praise and worship that reflects back from the throne room of God all the way to our hearts, then bounces back to soar through the heavenlies and arrive back at His feet in His throne room once again!

Worship is not about talent, or gifts. Worship is about heart, your heart resounding back to the Father God. The Lord God judges our hearts, our motives, and our intentions. Worship is not about the worshiper; worship is about the One being worshiped! When we get our perspectives reversed, then we worship backwards, and we create a distortion that is not unlike backwards masking, with a hidden message within our sound waves that says, "Look at me! I'm a worshiper!" Instead of "Look to God! He is the only One who deserves any praise or worship! Give it all to Him!"

As a worshiper this will be your greatest struggle for the rest of your life. It gets easier the more you deal with yourself but it will never go away, that desire to be seen and heard, that desire to be on the 'stage'. But you can bring it to the feet of the Father God, literally every time you come before Him. You can give Him that thought, that action, that 'thorn in your flesh' that everyone deals with, but never really talks about . . . you can give it to Him. If you don't deal with it now, it will cost you for the rest of your life and even into eternity.

What keeps you from going all the way into the Holy of Holies? What is that nagging thing in your mind that constrains your heart and holds you back? Is it pride masked as 'poor self- image'? Is it pride masked as humility? What is it? Is it a broken place from your past that tries to disqualify you every time you step up to take your place as His chosen worshiper? Take a moment to consider, pray and seek His face, and then write it down. Write it all down as it comes to you. This is your book; these are your notes, so say what you mean, and mean what you say. Write it all out for the Lord. Then lay it all down at His feet and leave it forever from this day forth.

_____

_____

_____

_____

_____

_____

_____
_____
_____
_____
_____
_____
_____
_____

In the early 1990's I had a conversation with an angel that changed my thinking forever concerning my personal worship. I was told by the angel to write down what he was about to tell me, so this is what I wrote, "You have often wondered why we appear at different times in the service. We are released to come in when the praise becomes pure. Not when you think it is pure, but when God knows it is pure by the hearts of the people. Then we are allowed to come in and do our jobs."

Our hearts are what God is always watching, listening to, and judging. Our hearts can be impure and yet we can look and sound pure to people around us. But God knows our hearts. We can even wear a mask from ourselves; we can hide so well that our own brain does not detect the flawed thinking that can stop the flow of true worship from within us. Many times pride masks itself as humility, but there are ways to check yourself, and your heart to make sure your motives are pure.

(Ezekiel 28) We must guard against the Luciferian spirit that cost the archangel of worship his highest-ranking position of worship for eternity! Lucifer lost his position because the sin of pride was found in him! If God were to look inside your heart today, what sin would He find in you? He is looking right now into your heart. What is keeping you from going all in with Him? What is keeping you from jumping into the deepest parts of His presence and becoming fully immersed in His glory? Let's stop for a moment and examine our own hearts. Now write down those things you can identify through this prayer time that you feel have held you down, and kept you out of the fullness of His presence and the ordination of your calling to be a true heart worshiper?

_____
_____
_____
_____
_____
_____
_____

He always knows our hearts, even when we don't know our own motives. He always knows our conscious and our subconscious thoughts! He will release whatever it is we need to lay down at His feet. That will help us go to the next level, the next position in the eternal realm of living and being worship. It is, and it always will be about the pureness of who we are. The pureness of our worship is a sure sign of the level of the pureness of our sacrifice to Him on the altars of our own lives of worship. What are you willing to give Him to get what you need to go fully into the Holy of Holies as a pure worshiper with a pure heart?

_____
_____
_____
_____
_____

The definition of worship in the Greek is the word 'proskuneo'. It means 'to prostrate oneself, bow down, do obeisance, show reverence, do homage, worship, adore. It also means 'homage rendered to God and the ascended Christ'. But my favorite is the simplest of the meanings. It means to 'kiss toward'. So when we are worshiping God in spirit and in truth, with pure hearts toward Him, it's as if we are blowing kisses toward Him! We are running toward Him, but we are not quite there yet, but we can't hold our worship any longer! I may not be right in Your face yet, and I may not be close enough to throw my arms around You yet, but as I run toward You, I will blow kisses toward Your face! I pursue You! I pursue Your presence! I long to worship You!

The Bible says in John 4 that God the Father searches the whole earth over for those who will worship Him in spirit and in truth. We will discuss exactly what does that mean in our generation; and what does that sound like and look like in our modern day settings of church worship?

Take a moment to write down anything else you feel the Lord is revealing to you about your own personal and private worship. We can never do publicly what we won't do privately. Worship begins in your bedroom, bathroom, living room, kitchen, and yes, even in your car. Worship begins in your alone time with Him. Worship begins in your conversations during your quiet time when it is just the two of you. So what else can you give Him? Write it down.

_____
_____
_____
_____
_____
_____
_____
_____

When a worshiper leaves the platform after the music portion of the worship service the questions of the mind should never be:
Did I lead the people in worship?
Did I do well?
Did I sing beautifully?
Did I play my instrument accurately?
Did I dance, or do drama, or art, or paint, or whatever expression of art you use to call it worship?
For at this point, the attention should never be on you! Never! These are the questions answered during practice, during rehearsals, during the 'study to show

yourself approved' times. When you leave the platform the questions that you should be asking are:

Did I worship God in spirit and in truth?

Did I touch the throne of God?

Did I touch the hem of His garment?

Did I abandon my desire to please humanity and only please my Creator?

Did He hear the sound of my worship so high in the spirit that only my Bridegroom could know the sound of His bride?

Did I sing as if no one was listening?

Did I dance as if no one was watching?

Did I use every fiber of my being: spirit, soul, and body, to worship the King of kings without the constraints of worrying what any human might think or say?

It remains the same. Worship is about the One being worshiped. It has never truly been nor will it ever be about the worshiper. There is no such thing as a 'worship leader', because no one can make me worship. You can't lead me to worship. You can only worship. If you worship in spirit and truth, I may follow you there. But you can't make me come to His throne. You can't cause me to worship. You can't lead me to worship. You may sing the 'lead'; you may 'lead music' but worship is about heart, my heart to God's heart, and God's heart to my heart. It's personal and private and holy and pure. Anything else is simply some other form of performance. God did not say in His word that He is looking for, searching the whole earth over for the best talent, the greatest giftings. If so, God would hover over places, like Hollywood, Las Vegas, and Broadway in New York City.

He met the woman at the well in Samaria in John 4. Where was the band? Where were the singers? There were none. There was only heart. When it all comes down to it, that's all He is ever looking for. Blessed are the pure in heart, for they shall see God! (Matthew 5:8)

What part of your worship needs the purifying fire of God's presence? Ask Him to show you and then write it down here and give it to your Lord.

_____
_____
_____
_____
_____
_____
_____
_____
_____
_____
_____

*Read Chapter One in the We Who Worship Book and answer the questions at the end of the chapter.

Chapter Two
Worship in Spirit

Since Jesus told the woman at the well two specific requirements to have the kind of worship that the Father seeks I feel we should explore both. Worshiping in spirit can only mean what it says. This is heart-to-heart, communion with the Father God. No flesh involved; I call this Holy of Holies kind of pure worship. I can see how the tabernacle was laid out with three levels of purification. The outer court experience was to rid us of our flesh, bringing it under to the will and purpose of God. The inner court was to bring our soul realm into submission so our minds, wills, and emotions are not still in control of our lives. Once we get to the entrance of the Holy of Holies, we should be pure enough to step into spirit worship without the hindrances of flesh and soul. We should be repentant of both levels of sin in our lives so that we can stand without fear of unrepentant sin in His presence.

Can you think of things in your flesh and soul realm (mind, will, and emotions) that need to be repented of, and receive forgiveness from the Father God through Jesus Christ our Lord and Savior? Write it down and get rid of it forever. Lay it at His feet and let it go, every mental, emotional, and physical thing that has held you; today is the day to turn it loose forever.

_____

_____

_____

_____

The word 'spirit' in John 4 in the Greek is translated from the word, 'ruach'. It means, 'spirit, wind, breath'. When we worship God in spirit, we are literally yielding our own spirits to His spirit, and we are experiencing a personal Acts 2 moment on our own! We give God our very breath and allow Him to play us for His glory without fear, or embarrassment, or anything else that would cause us to hold back. We simply yield.

When we yield ourselves to be played by His Spirit through our spirits when we worship, those who are present with us can be healed, refreshed, restored, and renewed. When King Saul was troubled by an 'evil spirit' David would play and worship God and the troubling spirit would leave him. When we can finally abandon our desire to perform, to be seen and heard, and fully yield to His Spirit while we worship, we can expect miracles to happen in every service. While we worship we should expect harassing spirits, infirmity spirits, sickness, disease, depression and oppression to flee! If we can truly worship Him in spirit we should be seeing literal signs and wonders happening all throughout the sanctuary while we worship!

What do you feel you could do better to attain this spiritual goal while you worship?

_____

_____

_____

How can you teach your team of worshipers to reach for this kind of deeper worship in spirit?

_____

_____

_____

In Philippians 3:3-4 the scripture states that "We are the circumcision, who worship God in the Spirit, rejoice in Christ Jesus, and have no confidence in the flesh, though I also might have confidence in the flesh. If anyone else thinks he may have confidence in the flesh, I more so:"

Paul is plainly stating that we should have no confidence in the flesh when we worship God. We cannot have confidence in our talent, or our gifts. We must only be circumcised, which is the removing of flesh! When we enter our music worship time in a service in our own ability we are totally relying on our flesh. We should never enter worship without much prayer, even fasting on some level to keep our flesh under. We should never rely on our talents, or gifts, or personalities, or even the times we have rehearsed. Oh, we should rehearse, and be the very best we can be for His glory. He deserves the best we can give Him, but we should never ever rely on it.

So we can do nothing wrong once we actually enter into worship. It is not the time to get upset with ourselves or others if a note is missed or a phrase is not perfect. Those things are dealt with in rehearsals, but never ever on the day we are actually worshiping our King. Don't allow the enemy to cause you to be self-focused even in a negative way. Don't allow the enemy to beat you up in your thoughts of not being good enough. Let me settle that right now for you. None of us are ever good enough to be in the Holy of Holies. That's why Jesus had to come to pay the price once and for all for us. We stand in His presence to worship Him simply because Jesus died for us and gave us access. We can't earn our way in . . . ever! So stop trying and enjoy the access you have been granted because of Jesus. Just accept it and stop performing for approval.

What lies of the enemy do you have to combat every time you go before the throne of God to worship Him?

_____

_____

_____

_____

Spirit worship is higher than mere singing or playing songs. Spirit worship is pure love toward the Father of love. Sometimes it is in our native language and other times there are no words at all. Sometimes pure spirit worship is silence at His feet. Sometimes spirit worship is dance, or drawing, or painting, or singing, or playing with no words. Sometimes it is an indefinable place we find within His presence that is so completely intimate with the Lover of your soul that it cannot be heard or seen by another human being.

What things have you experienced in your personal worship that you now realize must have been a moment when you tapped into real true spirit worship? Can you put it into words at all?

_____
_____
_____
_____
_____

When we worship in spirit others may follow, but they may not either. This one thing I have learned about worship even in a setting of many people, it's still personal and intimate and completely one-on-one. The harder I try to bring others with me, the less effective I am. If I will simply go into the Holy Place, some will come too. That's the best we can hope for at any given gathering of worshipers. So go in and discover the One who loves you without restraint. Learn from Him. The Holy Spirit will teach us how to worship the Father in spirit and in truth. He is the only One who can teach us, lead us, and direct us. Let's follow the Spirit of God and learn how to abandon our preconceived ideas of what worship really looks like and sounds like. He knows us far better than we know ourselves. He knows who we really are created to be forever. Teach us Holy Spirit how to worship our King!

What ways can you think of that you can implement right away that will help you hear the Holy Spirit better before you begin to sing, or play, or dance, or do a skit? What will help you be a more intimate spirit worshiper? Ask the Holy Spirit right now to show you what you need to know! Write it down.

_____
_____
_____
_____
_____
_____
_____
_____
_____
_____
_____
_____
_____
_____
_____
_____
_____
_____

Chapter Three
Worship in Truth

John 4:23 (Message Bible)

It's who you are and the way you live that count before God. Your worship must engage your spirit in the pursuit of truth. That's the kind of people the Father is out looking for: those who are simply and honestly themselves before him in their worship. God is sheer being itself – Spirit. Those who worship him must do it out of their very being, their spirits, their true selves, in adoration.

I could not have said it better myself. If we are going to obey the words of Jesus and worship God in spirit and truth, then we must literally engage our spirit in the pursuit of truth. God is truth. We must pursue Him, His very presence. That word 'engage' is one we must examine in our lives. Many times we just go through the motions of worship, singing or playing a prepared song, making all the right sounds, singing all the right words, and yet we are totally dis-engaged. God requires us to engage in our worship toward Him.

Truth. Jesus said in John 14:6, "I am the way, the truth, and the life." So to worship the Father in real truth means we must worship Him through His Son, Jesus. Without truly knowing Jesus intimately how can we worship Him in truth? What are some things, places in your mind, that more light of His presence could be presented to cause you to operate in even more truth when you worship Him? Nothing hidden, nothing missing, this is true worship. The only things the enemy can use against us are those things we won't allow into the light of God. His truth can set us free, even from our own minds. His truth can stop the enemy's assault on our thinking because of secrets, unresolved emotional issues, things we allow to stay in the dark of our minds. His truth can bring all of that into the light and can cause us to be able to truly worship Him at a higher and more truth-filled level. "Come up higher," says the Spirit of God . . . says the Spirit of Truth. "I will show you who you really are inside of Me," says the Lord.

I discuss at great length what the ancient Hebrew word for truth is in the original language. It is defined as 'that which nurtures or mothers the covenant'. Truth mothers covenant. Truth protects covenant. So when there is division, strife and confusion within the 'worship team' truth is not in operation, because truth will protect covenant. Truth never divides. Truth reconciles. Truth protects and brings to a resolution. Truth confronts everything. Truth hides nothing. Truth is God and God is truth. Jesus is truth and truth is Jesus. So when the Father looks for worshipers who worship in spirit and in truth, we must always be in constant check of our own motives and emotions. Truth never separates. Truth confronts, deals with, and reconciles all things.

What things have you allowed in your own worship, in your own life that is not truth? Let's deal with it and lay it down so we can worship Him in spirit and in truth.

_____
_____
_____

Fear in ancient Hebrew means 'without mothering'.   What fears have you allowed to live inside your mind, heart, and emotions that can be covered with the love and truth of God? Perfect love casts out fear. Love covers a multitude of sins.   Let's get it all out and deal with every hidden thing.   Just identifying what these fears are and writing them down can help you, with the Holy Spirit, to deal with them and bring them into the truth of God's love, forgiveness, and truth.

_____
_____
_____
_____
_____
_____
_____

Some of the greatest and most truthful worship I have ever experienced has happened since I have completely rid my being of fear. I know the devil can't kill me.   There is no fear anymore of somehow the enemy overpowering me and killing me before God is finished with me here.   God can't lose and the devil can't win.   Therefore, what do I have to fear? If the devil could have killed me he would have done it by now. He has had more than enough opportunities to do so, and yet, I'm still here to fulfill this last days' purpose from the throne of God to raise up worshipers with pure hearts for His glory.

Laying down my greatest fear and accepting that no matter what happens on this earth I will not be moved; I will never stop worshiping God; I will never stop serving God! This is a great revelation for me. I may not be able to take the 'gun out of the devil's hand' but this truth has most certainly allowed me to take all his bullets away!   When we buried our daughter, the great fear of my life was that the devil could kill my other children, or my husband or myself. I have settled all of this now.   The devil cannot touch any of us as long as we walk in truth and spirit. If we cross over to heaven, God allowed it. Never doubt that.   As long as we walk in His presence, the enemy cannot touch us.   Even though going to heaven before we get old, would be hard for those left behind, we have proven, we can go on. We have already done it. We know we can survive. And we can overcome. We are still here; we are still serving God. We are still worshiping God and we always will until our last breath here, and then we will worship Him forever with eternal breath!!!

What is your greatest fear?   Can you give it to Him now? Can you trust Him at the highest of levels? Can you tell God that you trust Him even with (you fill in the blank)?

_____
_____
_____

From the view of heaven looking down upon created mankind, when our worship is more about the worshiper than about the One being worshiped, then there is not even the slightest resemblance to truth. God is standing up in heaven, searching the whole earth over to you. He is looking to see if you are really ready to give it all to Him, to worship Him in spirit and in truth. Are you ready? He's been waiting a very long time to play you for His glory. He wants to show you who you really are. He wants to play the sounds of His presence, His breath blowing through your woodwind instrument, making a glorious sound of heaven to the earth, all coming forth from your being. Can you give Him your instrument? Will you give Him yourself?

Pure in heart is a powerful position to be in with God. The more pure our hearts become, the more open our eyes are to see Him! The more pure we are the more we reflect who He really is inside of us. The purer we become the less of us is seen and heard and the more of Him is seen and heard! The closer we are to His presence, the purer our hearts become. If you want to hear His still, small voice, you must come close! Come so close He can whisper in your ear. He can only tell you a secret when you get into the secret position . . . His mouth is upon your ear. His face is upon your face. His breath is mingled with your breath. He has your voice, your tongue, and your breath. He has your body, soul, and spirit. Are you ready? Come away with Him. He will show you who you really are inside of Him.

Turn loose of everything that has prevented you from the deepest of worship, the deeper things of God. Can you hear His voice right now? What is He saying to you?

_____
_____
_____
_____
_____
_____
_____
_____
_____
_____
_____
_____
_____
_____

What would you like to say to Him, the very Lover of your soul?

_____
_____
_____
_____
_____
_____
_____

Chapter Four
Guard the Heart of Worship

Most creative people must guard against being moved more by their emotions rather than by the spirit of God. Emotions can lie to us and make us think things that are not the truth. We must keep our hearts protected even from our own emotions.

Discouragement and disappointment can be huge enemies of our personal worship. If we allow our minds to entertain these two spirits of discouragement and disappointment they can quickly turn into great enemies of our worship. Soon if not dealt with, these two enemies can turn into disobedience, rebellion, and stubbornness. Hold your emotions in check to the Spirit of God. Confess each day that you are unoffendable. You are a dead person walking around housed in flesh. You cannot have your feelings hurt, or your heart offended. Many worshipers have lost their positions because of offense. Unresolved emotions, and poor communication can cause worship to be ruined instead of rebuilt.

Read I Kings 19 about Elijah, Ahab, and Jezebel. Watch the interaction between the prophet and the Lord God. See the progression of Elijah's disappointment and discouragement.

What areas have you allowed discouragement and disappointment in your past to steal your worship and slow your progress of becoming a true worshiper of God?

_____
_____
_____
_____

What can you learn when you read chapter four 'Guard the Heart of Worship' as you notice the details of the prophet Elijah's journey? What could he have done differently that might have saved his ministry?

_____
_____
_____

In Elijah's journey and conversations with God what do you see as you read that he could have said that might have made a difference?

_____
_____
_____

In your opinion what was his first and biggest mistake?

_____
_____
_____
_____

The more I meditate on this story before the throne of God the more I see certain warnings by the Spirit of God to my own heart and mind. We must follow the Lord; we must not try to lead the Lord! Elijah was following the Lord right up to the point where he listened to Jezebel instead of to the Lord. Once he 'ran for his life' from a human being's threats, he was off track. Once he allowed self-preservation to take over, instead of trusting God like he had always done in the past, it cost him his future.

When we allow disappointment and discouragement to set up housekeeping in our minds, it leads to depression, isolation and then deep exhaustion. God was there to strengthen Elijah but Elijah would not give up his 'wounds' and his words helped him hold on to his pain. What was it that Elijah continued to say over and over again to the Lord?

_____
_____
_____
_____
_____
_____

I have come to learn when God does not change the question He is asking me, that I must change my answer back to Him! Elijah kept answering God with the same answer and it cost him his ministry, and his future on the earth. Elijah was a great starter but he did not finish well because someone else had to take over and finish his calling. That's not to say that his life did not count for something! Of course it did! It changed history and He is forever remembered, but if he could have gotten past his disappointment and discouragement just think what he could have done teamed up with his successor, Elisha! Hindsight is always 20/20!

God is purifying His called and appointed worshipers even as I write this. He is coming for a purified bride, who is a purified worshiper. The bride of Christ is not a separate entity to the worshiper. They are one and the same. His purified bride will worship Him in spirit and in truth. When we worship in spirit and in truth, spots and wrinkles on the body of Christ will be washed away, purified, and we will be made ready for His coming.

Let's say the wonderful prayer of David from Psalm 51:10-13 together.

Create in me a clean heart, O God, and renew a steadfast spirit within me. Do not cast me away from Your presence, and do not take Your Holy Spirit from me. Restore to me the joy of Your salvation, and uphold me by Your generous Spirit. Then I will teach transgressors Your ways, and sinners shall be converted to You. Selah. Pause and calmly think on those words for a minute or two.

As worshipers, we must guard our hearts and not be led by highs and lows of emotions. We must only be led by the Spirit of God and stay balanced within ourselves.

Chapter Five
A Prepared Worshiper

Let's read together Matthew 25:1-13

Then the kingdom of heaven shall be likened to ten virgins who took their lamps and went out to meet the bridegroom. Now five of them were wise, and five were foolish. Those who were foolish took their lamps and took no oil with them, but the wise took oil in their vessels with their lamps. But while the bridegroom was delayed, they all slumbered and slept. And at midnight a cry was heard: "Behold, the bridegroom is coming; go out to meet him!" Then all those virgins arose and trimmed their lamps. And the foolish said to the wise, "Give us some of your oil, for our lamps are going out." But the wise answered, saying, "No, lest there should not be enough for us and you; but go rather to those who sell, and buy for yourselves." And while they went to buy, the bridegroom came, and those who were ready went in with him to the wedding, and the door was shut. Afterward the other virgins came also, saying, "Lord, Lord, open to us!" But he answered and said, "Assuredly, I say to you, I do not know you." Watch therefore, for you know neither the day nor the hour in which the Son of Man is coming.

This is a warning to everyone, especially worshipers who have already been given much. We have talents, and giftings, and callings and they are without repentance, which means these things will not be taken from us. We are required by the Father God to keep ourselves ready, alert, active, and awake! Notice in the verses above that they all had oil. They were all virgins. They all had lamps, and they all had oil. But only half of the group had ENOUGH oil. Notice that all ten were waiting for the bridegroom. Notice that all ten slumbered and slept. All slumbered and slept. At midnight they all heard the cry to go out and meet Him! They all arose and trimmed their lamps. Why did they need to trim their lamps? Because when a lamp burns for a while, the burned wick needs to be trimmed to make a clean wick to burn. If not trimmed, there is more smoke and less light.

This is where we have grown in the generation we are living in right now. We have too much untrimmed wick, and we produce too much smoke and not enough fire and light. Trimming the wick is like a circumcision of our flesh, our minds, our thinking, our souls, and even our spirits. We must continue to stay trimmed if we are going to be able to stand in His presence and be ready for His coming.

Can you think of areas in your life that need a good trimming? Why not list them here and as you write them down, lay them at His feet, inviting the Spirit of God to come in and cut away those areas in your life that need a good trimming.

_____
_____
_____
_____
_____

The word 'trimmed' in the Greek is the word 'kosmeo' and it means 'cosmetic, to beautify, arrange, decorate, furnish, embellish, adorn, and put in order'. What things in your life need to be put in order before you can truly become a worshiper at your highest level? What things have you allowed to go 'unnoticed' by others but your own heart condemns you every time you go to the platform to worship God?

_____

_____

_____

_____

_____

The number 'ten' means, 'responsibility, law, and testimony, the whole being, the entire group'. It is our responsibility as worshipers of the most high God to keep ourselves ready, trimmed, prepared, without spot or wrinkle. We must guard our hearts, and lives. We must keep watch over our own souls. It is so easy to become complacent, just going through the motions of a 'worship service'. It is especially easy to just check out when weekly multiple services are a part of our schedules. But here in this scripture we are commanded to keep watch! Watch for your own weaknesses to creep in, and cause your lamps to start to dim and go out. Keep watch that you keep enough and more than enough oil to be in your lamp so you don't get caught without enough sustaining oil. It is not about having oil; it's about having enough oil! All ten of the virgins had oil, but only five had enough oil!

Notice that the original oil as far as we can tell was freely given to them, but when they waited too late to get the 'free oil', the five that did not have enough oil had to go and buy for themselves! Go to those who sell, and buy for yourselves! When it all comes down to it, I am only responsible for myself, for my own level of oil. I want to take on your lives, your worship, your responsibility, but in the long run, I can't. I am only responsible for my own oil, keeping it full. Where in your own life of worship could you benefit from rebuilding and restoring, refilling the oil in your own life? Where have you allowed thinking, acting, and the being of your own person to get lax and cause you to grow cold and lose some very valuable and precious oil from your lamp? Be honest and as you write things down, take the time to repent before the Father.

_____

_____

_____

_____

_____

_____

_____

_____

_____

_____

This is the most in-your-face scripture to me in the New Testament because of the door being shut while the five were away buying the much-needed oil. This is a huge warning that time is short, and we cannot gamble with our lives, our eternal futures. We, who love God, can actually miss the rapture of the bride being taken with the bridegroom. I am not saying that the five that didn't have enough oil will miss heaven and eternity with Jesus forever. I cannot be certain of that, but the scripture is very plain that half of what we would call the modern day church will be left behind simply because they will not have kept enough oil in their vessels. After the five virgins bought oil, they came hurrying back, only to find the five that had enough oil were taken, and the door was shut! There may have been other seasons in history where time was their friend but now, in this season, we must stay ready, alert, and watching for His coming.

Watch therefore, for you know neither the day nor the hour when He is coming! He is coming! He is coming! Our worship should reflect this message. Our worship should have urgency to the lyrics and the melodies that causes each person present in the room to reflect, check, and examine his or her life. We must not get caught up in the time and season that besets our church society today of being sensitive to the 'seeker' so as not to offend or cause one to feel uncomfortable in the House of the Lord! I want you to feel uncomfortable. I want you to examine your hearts, minds, attitudes, actions, spirit, soul, and body. Take a good look at yourself in the light of His glory and see where you need to make changes. Then check your oil level; examine whether your 'wick' needs a good trimming and ask the Lord to start cutting away in those areas that hinder your worship. Help us, Lord!

Don't break the heart of the Lover of your soul. Don't make Him have to leave without you! Don't make Him have to close the door and have to speak the words, "I don't know you." You may know His name, but does He know your name? According to this scripture it is vitally important that He knows your name. Your earthly identity is of no consequence in the light of eternity. What kind of eternal identity are you making for Him, for His glory? What does He call you?

_____
_____
_____
_____
_____
_____

Lord, I long to be ready when You return for Your bride! Help me to become and to remain a prepared worshiper for Your glory and not my own!

_____
_____
_____
_____

Chapter Six
A Praying Worshiper

Psalm 46:10, "Be still and know that I am God."

There is only one I Am. He is the Lord. There is no other. In these last days of extremely busy lives, we must remember to 'still ourselves' in His presence and remember that who we are, what we do, and who we become is only about knowing who He is! When we know who He is, then we can easily begin to overcome our own flesh, broken places, and quirky thinking! Keeping our hearts and minds on Him, and Him alone, can straighten out even the most 'messed up' self-absorbed musician. Notice it did not say self-absorbed worshiper, because there is no such thing. A worshiper cannot be about the one worshiping, but rather the One being worshiped! Until we stop fidgeting in the flesh we can never truly know Him as the great I Am!

This will take discipline on your part as a worshiper. This means you cannot simply play music, or sing a song and call yourself a worshiper. You must learn to pray, and spend private time alone, and still with the great I Am. This is more than just gaining knowledge or revelation. This is about simply 'being' with the One who created you, without having to 'get something, or hear something.' This is about getting comfortable in His presence, so when you try to actually help others find their way to the inner Holy of Holies of their personal worship you have actually been there on a regular basis yourself!

Take a moment to write God a few lines of a song only for Him. Just write what comes out of your heart right now. Write down the lyrics of your soul. This is for His ears only so don't hold back. Tell Him who He is in your life. Tell Him what your heart longs to sing to Him. This is not for others to hear. You are not performing; you are simply worshiping the Author and Finisher of your being. Sing to Him. Write it down.

_____
_____
_____
_____
_____
_____
_____
_____
_____
_____
_____

Worshipers are created to worship. If you are doing anything other than worshiping, then you are wasting your time, and not fulfilling your destiny. Don't misunderstand me. Worshipers are worshiping no matter what they are 'doing'. If you have a job, while you are fulfilling the duties of that particular job, you are also worshiping the King, which means you fulfill every task set before you with integrity, honor, and accountability. Everything you 'do' you do it with the utmost desire to be as good as you possibly can, and you do it as unto our God in worship. Cleaning the bathroom, doing laundry, working in the garden, and the fields all those years of my growing up life, is actually where I learned to be a true worshiper! The platform is where we wind up as a worshiper but it is most certainly not where we start learning to worship!

I want you to answer the list below honestly before your God.

These are prerequisites of being a true worshiper.

A worshiper must:
Be saved. Are you saved? _____
Be filled with the Holy Spirit. Are you filled with the Holy Spirit? _____
Be surrendered to His presence? Are you surrendered? _____
Be crucified with Christ. Are you a dead person worshiping? _____
Be reconciled to God. Are you one with your creator? _____
Be holy. Are you living a holy life? _____
Be righteous. Are you robed in righteousness every minute? _____
Be forgiven. Have you asked Him to forgive you and cleanse you? _____
Be humble. Are you continually bowed down before Him? _____
Be purified. Are you putting yourself in the Fire of His Presence? _____
Be clean and made ready. Are you clean and ready for His coming? _____
Be submitted and obedient. Are you submitted and obedient? _____
Be all about the Lord. Are you living your life all about Him or are you still about you?

_____

Notice that the one word that is the same is 'BE'. We are a church society all hung up on what we 'do' but God is more interested in our being, and who we are inside of His presence.   The more we spend time with Him, the more we pray, and stay on our knees and on our faces in His presence the more we are prepared to be true worshipers of the most high God.   We cannot make ourselves ready to stand in His presence but His presence can make us ready! His presence can reveal things that are hidden in our hearts, even hidden from us!

Learn to pray like Jesus prayed in John 17:1-26.   As you open your Bible and read this entire passage what can you see that Jesus did that can be applied to your life daily as you pray?

_____
_____
_____
_____
_____
_____
_____

What kinds of worship prayers have been neglected that we can instill in these last days?   What did Jesus do when He prayed that we don't see or hear anymore?

In Matthew 6:9-13 Jesus plainly called heaven to earth when He prayed, 'Your _____ come! Your _____ be done, on _____ as it is in _____'. Calling heaven to earth through our worship is very important in these last days. Jesus is coming and it is getting perilous here. We must have more heaven on earth to survive the things that are distracting us from walking and living and being pure before Him.

Romans 8:26-28 in the Message Bible, "Meanwhile, the moment we get tired in the waiting, God's Spirit is right alongside helping us along. If we don't know how or what to pray, it doesn't matter. He does our praying in and for us, making prayer out of our wordless sighs, our aching groans. He knows us far better than we know ourselves, knows our pregnant condition, and keeps us present before God. That's why we can be so sure that every detail in our lives of love for God is worked into something good."

Don't you just love how the Bible states that we are pregnant with worship? We are pregnant with the Spirit of God ever wanting to pray through us. Even when we can't put into words what we want to pray, or sing, or worship before the throne of God, the Spirit of God will pray, sing, and worship through us!!! How awesome to think that we can be played like an instrument for His glory! Let's take a moment to be still and pray without words. Be still and groan in wordless sighs and aching groans, allowing the Spirit of God to pray, sing, and worship through you right now! After you have finished this time with Him using you in this way write down what you have experienced, for His eyes-only!

_____
_____
_____
_____
_____
_____
_____
_____
_____

Lord, I give myself to You, completely. Your word states in I Corinthians, 14:15, ". . . I will pray with the spirit and I will also pray with the understanding. I will sing with the spirit, and I will also sing with the understanding."

Have you experienced praying and singing in both your natural language and your heavenly language? _____
If not, why? _____

Acts 2: 4 states that 'they were all filled with the Holy Spirit and began to speak with other tongues, as the Spirit gave them utterance.' Why not ask Him to use you, to fill you with His presence right now? Step over into His full control, and let go of those broken places within you that have kept you from being completely His! Do you trust Him even with your voice, your sound, and your worship? _____

You want to be a worshiper, then you must first learn how to be an intercessor, how to pray and stay in prayer. Consistency in your prayer life is what will keep you clean and pure before Him. If you can't take the time to pray, then stay off the platform, and stop calling yourself a worshiper. If you want to be a true worshiper, then learn to be still and stay at His feet until you get over yourself to become all about Him!

Worship is a high calling, with many temptations. Pride is the most obvious one, and yet many times, the hardest to spot in our own lives. It's so easy to see when someone else puts on the mantle of pride and takes off the covering of humility but in our own lives, it's very hard to see. Pride hides from the one it is trying to cover. We must have the eyes of the Spirit of God to even see clearly. Our own eyes deceive us. True wisdom is not about age; true wisdom comes from spending time in the presence of almighty God. The Bible states that humility is the beginning of wisdom. Wisdom is birthed on our knees, ever pushing 'self' out of our lives.

We must lay down our need to be noticed; we must lay down our need for approval and realize that God, our Father, has already approved us when He created us!

What things inside your thinking do you need to lay down to be completely used by the Father God? Are you His instrument or are you still trying to play your own sound, your own ideas of what worship within you really is?

_____
_____
_____
_____
_____
_____
_____
_____
_____
_____
_____
_____
_____

The rote repetition of words is not what true prayer is. God's kind of prayer is touching heaven, and allowing heaven to touch us! In what ways can you think of that you can allow heaven to touch you personally when you pray?

_____
_____
_____
_____
_____
_____

Chapter Seven
A Humble Worshiper

This is a given in true worship. If you are not humble then you are not a worshiper. Worship in the purest of forms is all about the One being worshiped and not about the 'worshiper'. The worshiper is all about the One, and has nothing left within them that would not be 'bowed down' before the One. Anything less than this is performance and performance is the exact opposite of worship. Performance is about the performer; worship is about the One being worshiped.

All pride must go. There have been times in my life when the Lord has required different things of me to 'kill' the pride within me. I lost my voice for a whole year in the early '90's and I had to discover other ways to express my personal daily worship. The more I got over myself and used methods that I was not as gifted in to worship the Lord, like dancing before Him, and clapping my hands in rhythms of praise, the more I 'died' to myself. It was a hard few months for me, but some of my most productive times before the Lord. I did not have my 'gifts' to rely upon, but had to utilize other methods to achieve higher worship before the throne of God.

What gifts and talents have you automatically relied on to worship the Lord?

_____
_____
_____

If you lost the ability to use those gifts, or were unable to use them for a period of time, what could you do to worship the Lord in other ways?

_____
_____
_____
_____
_____

Two scriptures that can help us see how much the Lord loves humility is the last line of Psalm 9:12, "... He does not forget the cry of the humble."

And in Psalm 10:17, "Lord, You have heard the desire of the humble; You will prepare their heart; You will cause Your ear to hear."

Sometimes our worship may not be a beautiful, lyrical, melodic sound but simply a cry of the humble heart. God promises in His word that He will cause His ear to hear a humble and prepared heart. What areas of your life could be worked on to make sure you are humble enough to worship Him? What things have you still to work on in which you rely more on giftings and talents instead of your humble heart?

_____
_____
_____

Jesus will always deal with our hearts and keep us in the right place of humility if we are continually in His face asking Him to help us. We must keep ourselves bowed low before Him if we are to stay in our rightful position of worship. I long for the days when we are able to face worshipers toward the altar, with our backs to the congregation.

When I first began to deal with my own pride of performance during the times I called 'worship' I began to realize that it was an ongoing continual battle to not think about myself while I was worshiping God! What an oxymoron that statement is! And yet, there it was, a huge battle began to keep my mind on Him, and to not think about myself, my own singing, my playing, my appearance, my sound! I had done the same exact things in my mind for many years but it was not until I realized what I was doing that it became sin!

To him who knows to do right and does not do it, to him it is sin! (James) Up until the moment that I realized what I was doing, every moment before that was just ignorance at best. But after I realized and had full knowledge that my heart was lifted up, from that moment on I was expected to 'deal with myself' and get rid of every thought of 'self' and get my thoughts in line to only think on Him!

When I first began to deal with my own uplifted heart in pride, I wanted to get on my face and stay on my face to keep from being lifted up. In the beginning I spent a lot of time completely bent over, and even flat on the floor at times. Some people thought I had lost my mind, but the fact is, I was losing my pride. We must do what we have to do to deal with ourselves at these times, and moments of realization. Up until this moment when you stand before the people to worship, what thoughts have been allowed to rule within you?

_____
_____
_____
_____
_____

What physical things can you think of that you might be able to do to bring your own pride under and bring about a humble heart to be birthed within you?

_____
_____
_____
_____

Repent in the ancient Hebrew means to 'burn the past to the ground'. The literal visual image painted in words means that true repentance means there is nothing left of yourself, your thoughts, your past victories or defeats that should be able to steal your thought life. Once repentance is truly accomplished you have a clean slate to begin your journey forward. There is nothing left within you, no memory great enough, no moment of either defeat or victory that can overshadow this moment in time when you stand before God almighty, alone with the most high God, as you worship Him in spirit and in truth.

The greatest of all promises within the scriptures for one who is striving to obtain humility lies within the promises of Psalm 147:6, "The Lord lifts up the humble; He casts the wicked down to the ground."

If you simply see the opposite phrases you will quickly be able to notice that the opposite of 'humble' is 'wicked'. God will Himself lift up the humble, but God Himself will cast the wicked down to the ground. Satan has first-hand experience with being cast down to the ground, and it was as a pride-filled head of worship, worshiper, that his sin of pride was discovered within him, and caused him to lose his God -given position in heaven as worshiper! We must continually be examining our own hearts to make sure 'pride is not found in us'. If you carefully examine Ezekiel 28 you will discover that pride was found in him. It was not always in him, but was found later on within him. We are the keepers of our own hearts, minds, attitudes, and actions. We must continually guard ourselves to make sure that what was once pure within us, does not 'turn' somewhere along the way to pride.

What ways can you think of to help yourself to make sure that pride is not found within you?

_____

_____

_____

_____

Matthew 18:4 states, "Therefore whoever humbles himself as this little child is the greatest in the kingdom of heaven."

The phrase 'humbles himself' should be what jumps off the page of this scripture. It is my job to keep myself humble. It is your job to keep yourself humble. What methods of daily service before the Lord help you stay humble and at His feet?

_____

_____

_____

_____

_____

In this particular scripture the word 'humble' is the Greek word 'tapeinoo' which literally means 'to make low'. It is used in reference to a mountain in Luke 3:5. Metaphorically, the word means, 'to debase, humble, lower oneself.' It is described as 'a person who is devoid of all arrogance and self-exaltation – a person who is willingly submitted to God and His will'.

What areas of your life still remain, that could be submitted to His will and to His plan and purpose? Can you write them out here and finally give them to Him? Can you trust Him with these last few areas of submission?

_____

_____

_____

_____

_____

Chapter Eight
A Pure Worshiper

You will notice in the We Who Worship book that I have listed many scriptures dealing with personal purity. A plea for purity is being sent forth from the throne room of God to His people. We must put ourselves within the very fire of His presence if we are going to sustain the level of purity that it takes to continually stand in His presence and worship Him. This is a journey of purification, realizing that the only time we actually enter into the destiny of purity is once we shed this earth body and walk eternally free from flesh. But this is no excuse to stay the way we are. Hardly! This is a warning and a challenge to deal with us daily before His presence to continually walk in oneness with His Spirit.

This is about keeping our hearts and minds in a place of purity. Our actions will follow what our hearts choose. We cannot walk in purity in the natural until we have laid it all at His feet daily and submit our personal beings to His purification process. I cannot purify myself. I can only accept what He has done for me to give me the opportunity to walk in unity with Him.

With our God it is all or nothing. He does not want a part of us, but all of us. He does not want us in 'word' but not in 'deed'. Our actions will always follow our choices. Purity is about our being. Our being must choose to 'be holy' even as He is holy. We live in a society that has many excuses for impure actions, motives, and hearts. But God never changes. He expects and requires holiness if we are to stand in His presence.

Purity and holiness are choices. We must personally choose to walk in purity and holiness. It is not a multiple choice test where we can say yes to the blessings of God, but no to liviving pure and holy! It is all yes, or all no!

The scriptures are very plain and it can easily be seen what the Lord requires of us.

Psalm 18:26, "With the pure You will show Yourself pure . . . "

Proverbs 16:2, "All the ways of a man are pure in his own eyes, but the Lord weighs the spirits."

Proverbs 15:26, "The thoughts of the wicked are an abomination to the Lord, but the words of the pure are pleasant."

Psalm 29:2, "Give unto the Lord the glory due to His name; Worship the Lord in the beauty of holiness."

If we truly want to worship the Lord it must be in purity and holiness. He accepts nothing less. What areas of your life, your thinking, and your actions can you think of that could be purified even more so in His fire of purification?

_____
_____
_____
_____

Are you willing to give those areas to Him right now and submit to the 'fire of His presence'?

_____

_____

Are we going to mess up? Of course, we will make mistakes. We will fall and have to be forgiven, but we have an advocate with the Father through the blood of Jesus in I John 1:9 that allows us to continually keep our persons humbled before Him in a repentant state which allows purity and holiness to stay in the midst of our hearts.   This is not a license to sin, but rather a reminder that we cannot be pure on our own. This is a legal position that we have a right to because of what Jesus Christ has done for us. This is our advocate, our counselor, the One who always stands between us, and what we actually deserve!   Jesus took what we deserve so we can have what He deserves! What a Savior!

What do you deserve from your past life?

_____

What do we get instead?

_____

_____

You are God's called and appointed worshiper. This is your destiny. You were created, and designed from within your very cellular level to worship God in the beauty of holiness forever and ever! And you get to start here on this earth and then continue on into eternity!   What are you going to do with this awesome gift?   Are you going to walk this out and stop allowing the enemy's lies to stop you in your tracks?   The enemy has been stealing your destiny because of his disqualifying lies. Bring all the lies into the light of God's presence here on this page and stop the enemy today.   Make a list below of all the lies the enemy has used against you and as you write them out, allow the Holy Spirit to brand into your being the purification of His fire over each and every area. Can you do this? Mean it forever, and don't ever take this lie back into your mind, and heart again.

_____

_____

_____

_____

_____

_____

_____

_____

_____

_____

_____

Chapter Nine
A Worshiper of Integrity

Integrity. This is not a word we have heard much about in our present day society church. And yet it is an absolute prerequisite to stand in the very presence of God. We have so 'dumbed down' our church family so as not to intimidate the average 'church-goer' that we have completely put God Himself out of our services! God is not mocked! He will not tolerate a lukewarm society just because we want everyone to feel welcome! God's house is not a country club! God's house and the environment of God's house must cause us to closely examine ourselves in His presence. God's presence causes us to fall on our faces before an all-consuming fire and want to be different!

Psalm 26:11-12, "But as for me, I will walk in my integrity; redeem me and be merciful to me. My foot stands in an even place; in the congregations I will bless the Lord."

Integrity causes us to stand in an 'even place'. Which means a lack of integrity causes us to stand in an 'uneven place'. If we are not standing in an even place, stable and fixed we are not able to 'bless the Lord'! When our own integrity is in question we must examine ourselves closely in the light of His presence, and His forgiveness. We are incapable on our own to create a pure heart that is filled with integrity. In our own abilities we are filled with sin, incapable of redeeming one hair on our own heads! But because of what Jesus did for us we can retain our integrity because of His redemption and His mercy.

What does 'integrity' mean to you?

_____
_____
_____

Integrity can be gained over a lifetime but lost in a moment. What can you do to protect yourself and retain your integrity in the future?

_____
_____
_____
_____
_____

Proverbs 22:1, "A good name is to be chosen rather than great riches, loving favor rather than silver and gold."

Your name represents who you are, and what you are. Keeping your heart and your life before almighty God can help protect your name. What areas of your life can you see as you gaze into this scripture that need to be more protected?

_____
_____
_____

What areas of your life has the enemy tried to steal your integrity?

_____
_____
_____
_____
_____

Integrity cannot be bought. It must be sought by one whose heart is pure before the Lord. We must run after His presence if we are to keep ourselves pure and clean before Him.   It is a losing battle to try and protect yourself and your name without the power and presence of the Holy Spirit.   Once we realize that it is through Him, and for Him, and by Him, and in Him that we are all He has created us to be, that we can truly start retaining and retraining our integrity.

I Peter 3:12, " For the eyes of the Lord are upon the righteous (those who are upright and in right standing with God), and His ears are attentive to their prayer. But the face of the Lord is against those who practice evil [to oppose them, to frustrate, and defeat them]. (Amplified Bible)

I want the Lord's eyes to be upon me. Do you? I want Him to see my heart. I know better than anyone that without Him I am completely impure, and without any integrity at all.   My own heart condemns me without His presence and covering. But inside of His presence I am found ready. I want the Lord to be able to examine the fruit of my life and to see that with Him I am fruitful.

Mark 11:12-14, "Now the next day, when they had come out of Bethany, He was hungry. And seeing from afar a fig tree having leaves, He went to see if perhaps He would find something on it. When He came to it, He found nothing but leaves, for it was not the season for figs. In response Jesus said to it, 'Let no one eat fruit from you ever again.' And His disciples heard it."

This is a most interesting story of Jesus and this fig tree.   The fig tree is the only tree that fruits first. In other words, before it puts out leaves, it puts out fruit! We call these first fruits.   The first thing the fig tree does is it becomes fruitful! Many times we should examine our own lives and establish whether we are fruitful.   The first thing we should be in our daily lives is fruitful.   Once we have produced fruit then 'leaves' can be produced. What do leaves do for a tree? First of all, the leaves on a fig tree protect the fruit from the birds and other animals. If there are leaves to cover the fruit, then the fruit can remain until it is fully ripe. But if there are no leaves, then many times the fruit is eaten before it can come to its ripeness.

John 15:16 (NKJV), "You did not choose Me, but I chose you and appointed you that you should go and bear fruit, and that your fruit should remain, that whatever you ask the Father in My name He may give you."

Integrity helps you to be able to remain fruitful. Integrity helps your 'fruit to remain'. We are to go and bear fruit, and our fruit should remain!

But when Jesus went to the fig tree because He was hungry, and started looking within the leaves, He found no fruit.   When Jesus comes to you every day as you worship Him, does He find any fruit? Or does He simply find a lot of leaves?

Leaves are supposed to protect the fruit, but many times in our lives, all the leaves are doing is hiding the places of unfruitfulness. When the Lord examines your heart right now, will He find fruit that remains, or a lot of hiding places for unfruitful activity? Make a list of areas of your life where you have wasted a lot of unfruitful time and activities that will not last.

_____
_____
_____
_____

Write the Lord a letter below and tell Him where you need help, where you need to repent, and where you want Him to help you rebuild your integrity as a worshiper of the most high God.

_____
_____
_____
_____
_____
_____
_____
_____
_____
_____
_____
_____
_____
_____
_____
_____
_____
_____
_____
_____
_____
_____
_____
_____
_____
_____

Recognize that without His help we will never be able to retain our integrity or be able to stand in His presence. This very realization has always helped me stay completely dependent upon my God!

Chapter Ten
An Accountable Worshiper

Accountability is a word that rubs most worshipers the wrong way. We are gifted, highly talented people who like to be 'free spirits'. We don't normally like to have to answer to others! This is a huge flaw in the character of a worshiper and one that must be realized, to be used of the Lord for any length of time.

One of the main areas that have a constant turnover in church staffs is in the area of so-called 'worshipers'. The area of the arts department, whether it be music, drama, art, dance, etc. is the hardest to maintain a constant place of being rooted and planted in the house of the Lord. The artistic side of humanity is what we have so casually dismissed with phrases like, "Oh they are just musicians," or "These flighty attitudes come with the territory of their giftings." No! This ought not to be! We must discipline our own selves to stand, and stay. We must find ways to bring ourselves into accountability without the constant need for human approval, and validation.

Musicians, artists, drama, and dancers can be the most exhausting people to be around because of their constant need of human approval. We must take that need for approval and channel it into a position and a place of accountability. Once we can put ourselves and our talents and gifts at His feet and submit ourselves to the Father God and to the leadership in the house in which He has planted us, we will be able to deal with our own shortcomings more effectively.

Where you are most mentally attacked is usually where you need to be the most accountable. What are the overall lies the enemy hits you with as a musician, worshiper, etc?

_____

_____

_____

These are the areas where you need to become the most accountable. Your accountability and the recognition of your weaknesses in these areas will help you overcome the accuser of the brethren.

Matthew 5:23-24, "Therefore if you bring your gift to the altar, and there remember that your brother has something against you, leave your gift there before the altar, and go your way. First be reconciled to your brother, and then come and offer your gift."

I have read this scripture many times and I always had the mental thinking that my gift was my tithe, or my financial offering. But we have many gifts that we bring to the altar. Our worship is our gift; our talents are our gifts that we bring before Him. He states plainly in this scripture if you have something against someone, or if someone has something against you, don't even bother bringing your gifts to the altar until you go and settle this 'thing' that is between you and another person. Wow! So when we come before the Lord, week after week, with our gifts and talents and worship the king, He does not accept our worship, our gifts, because we have ought against someone else, or someone else has something against you! The Lord says to leave your gift at the altar, and go get the 'thing' settled between you and the other person. Then once it is settled then come back and offer your gift!

What or who do you have something against, or they have something against you?

_____
_____
_____

Have you gone to them and tried to settle it?

_____
_____

The Bible is very specific that it is our responsibility to work it out. This does not mean that we will always be best friends with everyone, but from our perspective, and from our end, our hearts, attitudes, and minds we have done our best to bring things to the best conclusion possible. Once you have done your part, no matter how they react, respond, then you can come and bring your gifts before the Lord. I cannot be responsible for the actions, words, or attitudes of another, but I am accountable to the Lord and before the Lord to keep my own heart and mind clean and prepared before Him. Can you say the same?

_____
_____

Please do not misunderstand me. I am not saying that you should always be in agreement with everyone around you. There will always be those in our lives with which we cannot agree. There will always be sin issues, doctrinal issues, and even personality differences that cause us to keep ourselves separate from certain ones. This is not what this scripture is talking about. And when you are honest with yourself you know exactly those areas where you 'hold on to your pride', and use excuse after excuse to 'feel the way, or respond the way, or act the way' you do toward particular individuals. It is these areas in which the Spirit of God is expecting us to deal personally with ourselves.

Accountability starts with my own person being honest with myself before my Father God. Then I must deal with my own heart and be daily accountable to the Spirit of God as He deals directly with me. Then I must get into God's house, and become accountable to a pastor who will give an account of me before the Father God.

Hebrews 13:17, "Obey those who rule over you, and be submissive, for they watch out for your souls, as those who must give account. Let them do so with joy and not with grief, for that would be unprofitable for you."

The Lord through His word has set it up that we should be accountable to those who we are submitted to, as those pastors, leaders, and parents are watching out for our souls, and they must give an account for us before the Lord. I see that the Lord says to make sure those who must give an account for us can do so with joy! Don't be the kind of person that when the Lord asks your pastor about your heart, the pastor has to 'sigh and be in grief' asking the Lord for more mercy for you. The Bible says that if those who must give an account for you have to do so with grief, then it is not profitable for you!

This all comes down to trust. We must learn to be submissive and accountable to those the Lord has put over us, and we must trust the Lord enough to know He will watch over every detail of our lives so that even when we do not agree with those over us, that when we submit to their authority and become submissive to what we are being told to do, that the Lord will take care of everything else. This all comes down to how much do we trust the Lord. Do we trust Him to the level that when we are sure we are doing the right thing and yet our leadership over us says do not do it that way that we trust the Lord to work it all out for our good? What areas is the Lord bringing to your memory right now that need to be laid at His feet, completely trusting that He will work it out if we will simply trust Him with the details?

_____
_____
_____
_____
_____

The enemy's roadblock to our personal and collective worship is broken relationships. We must examine our journeys, and if there is a long road of broken friendships, leadership, etc. in our past days, the only common denominator in all these relationships is us! What can you do differently in the future that can help you have less trouble and more peace? God's way to enter into His presence is to personally stay broken at His feet. I must keep myself in a continual state of broken pride, broken life, and a broken heart.

_____
_____
_____

As worshipers, we are accountable to the Spirit of God, then to leadership over us. We are not to 'hold our leadership' hostage by threatening to leave if they don't do such and such. If you want to leave, then leave! God will replace you! You are not irreplaceable. Lucifer was not irreplaceable! God made a whole race of people, called humans, to take his place. God can and will replace you when your heart becomes lifted up and you won't submit yourself to leadership and authority over you.

The only way you can stay ready to be used as a worshiper of the most high God is to be continually dealing with your own flesh, your own pride, and your own heart that desires to be lifted up. All worshipers deal with the same issues. It started in the throne room of God with the first worshiper and it is the continual enemy of all true worshipers. The only way to combat pride is accountability and submission. Don't resist it.

Chapter Eleven
A Submissive Worshiper

Ephesians 5:19-21, "Speak out to one another in psalms and hymns and spiritual songs, offering praise with voices [and instruments] and making melody with all your heart to the Lord, at all times and for everything giving thanks in the name of our Lord Jesus Christ to God the Father. Be subject to one another out of reverence for Christ (The Messiah, the Anointed One)." (Amplified Bible)

Submission is the most powerful tool of agreement. We must not come before the Father as a group of worshipers without being submitted one to the other, and also to our leadership. What is the mission of the house of God in which we serve? You must know the mission of the house and be in agreement with it if you are to serve submitted to that house. Then always check yourself and your heart toward the Father God. Where are you in submission to His will and purpose for your life?

We are God's instruments. We are to be so submitted to His will and purpose that we have no will or purpose or agenda of our own. This includes down to the very last details of each service. If the pastor asks you to change a song from your list, you obey. Just obey. Don't get all up in the air over it. It may not be about the song at all. It may simply be a test from the Lord of your willingness to obey leadership over you. Don't think that a song brings the anointing, because it doesn't. I am old enough and have been around long enough to know a wordless sigh or an aching groan can bring a glory of God down upon a house! It is not about lyrics, or melody. It is about the instrument's ability to be used, to be played, to be silent, to make noise! Whatever the Lord asks of you, do it!

As His worshipers, we must obey Him at all times. We do not belong to ourselves; we belong to Him. We do not have a plan, or a vision, or even a desire anymore. Our desires are His desires, our plans are His plans, and our vision is His vision. Until we get to this place inside of Him, we are of no eternal use to Him. You and I are not important here. He is the only one who is important. What He wants is what goes! What we want does not exist anymore!

We have been working through a lot of personal issues in these past pages so let's not stop until we have rid ourselves of it all. What plans, thoughts, ideas, and desires do you still need to lay at His feet to be able to walk completely and wholly as His own?

_____

_____

_____

_____

_____

_____

If we truly believe the Bible and want to be used to fulfill it, when was the last time you spoke to someone else in psalms and hymns and spiritual songs? The NT scripture states we are supposed to be doing just that! That means that new songs of the Spirit should be continually coming forth from our beings allowing us to speak to one another as worshipers! For some of us, this is our best way of communicating! When we have nothing else in common, we can worship together before the Lord. We can sing psalms, and hymns, and spiritual songs.

Let's take a minute to yield ourselves to this place. Be so submitted, so yielded to His presence, so 'dead to yourself' that He can play you for His glory and sing to someone else through your vocal instrument. For some, this will be your greatest pride test. Can you be a fool for Christ to the point of being used for His glory to speak to someone else?

We can do this in our worship but can you take this to the streets? Can you be used for His glory at the grocery store or the mall? I know you can, but you have to be willing to allow the Spirit of God to use you. Don't worry about it. It may not come out as a melody or a song to the one listening. It may sound like a simply a smile, with a 'hello' or a 'have a good day' or 'God bless you' attached to it. Being used by God will feel completely out of control on your end but on the recipient's end, it will just sound like 'love in action'.

Don't be too weird about being used for God's glory. Just yield yourself. He will do it through you. He is always accepted and received. Love covers a multitude of sins. Love never fails. Love casts out fear. Your submission to be used by the Spirit of God may feel like you have completely lost control but God will use you for His glory. Of this you can be sure. He does not want to make you look bad. In fact it is not about you at all! He wants to draw all men unto Himself, and He wants to use you to do that!

What ways can you allow the Spirit of God to use you when you are not on the platform in a service setting? How can you practice your submission levels in your daily routine?

_____
_____
_____
_____

Submission to the One who has created you is about agreeing with His plans and purpose. It is about agreeing so completely with who He has made you to be that you have no objections to anything He asks you to do! So how can I obtain this kind of training into my being? I Corinthians 14:15 gives us some of the best instructions of personal ways to grow in submission.

"Then what am I to do? I will pray with my spirit [by the Holy Spirit that is within me], but I will also pray [intelligently] with my mind and understanding; I will sing with my spirit [by the Holy Spirit that is within me], but I will sing [intelligently] with my mind and understanding also." (Amplified Bible)

There are two ways in which we can grow in the levels of submission. We grow by yielding first our spirits to God's Spirit. We allow the Spirit of God to pray through us using our breath, tongue, voice, to make the sounds of our heavenly language, but then we follow that up using our own minds to interpret what the Spirit of God is saying through us. We do this in prayer and in singing. This level of yielded submission will cause us to grow and become more useful to the Spirit of God.

Submission is one of the most powerful tools of the power of agreement. Submission must be a 'heart practice' first; then a mind, will, and emotions practice. Our persons will follow what our hearts choosen to do and be.

Is there anything else you need to lay at His feet before we go any further?
_____
_____
_____
_____

Submission is essential when multitudes gather to worship at His throne. When we are submitted to His will then we can flow by His Spirit and the great Conductor can orchestrate the sounds coming from all our different and unique instruments, causing perfect harmony and unity.

We have no will of our own; we are instruments within the orchestra. Only the One who plays us has any will. Many can operate as a unified being of worship when submission is in place in each individual and the Spirit of God is in full control.

We need more time in His presence, more time in preparation of learning how to yield our hearts to His will and purpose. I am not saying that rehearsals are not necessary. Of course, we are to be the best in the natural that we can be also. We are to prepare ourselves, our sounds, our voices, and instruments, our dances, art, etc. to be to the best of our abilities, but not at the expense of our submitted hearts. Our hearts must be yielded to His will and purpose to the same level of preparation as we have done in the natural realm of preparation. So pray in the natural and the spirit. Sing in the natural and the spirit. Utilize the Spirit of God in rehearsals to bring about unity and submission to the Spirit of God as a whole group, and individually as well. Don't forget to include all people involved, not just those on the platform. Sound, lighting, and media people are just as important to the unity of the group as any who may be seen on the platform, maybe even more so! Include everyone when praying, and flowing by the spirit in rehearsals, and prayer time together. Pray for each other. Pray for unity, for all to be anointed by the Spirit of God. Do not take lightly any task set forth within the group. All are important and must be submitted to His will and purpose.

Chapter Twelve
An Authoritative/Disciplined Worshiper

Proverbs 29:2, "When the righteous are in authority, the people rejoice; but when a wicked man rules, the people groan."

Matthew 28:18-20, "And Jesus came and spoke to them, saying, 'All authority has been given to Me in heaven and on earth. Go therefore and make disciples of all the nations, baptizing them in the name of the Father and of the Son and of the Holy Spirit, teaching them to observe all things that I have commanded you; and lo, I am with you always, even to the end of the age.' Amen."

To be the kind of worshiper with authority and discipline, we must be hidden inside Christ's identity. He is the 'all authority' we are to stand within. Authority is a powerful tool in the right hands and it causes many to flourish when the right leadership is in proper positions. This is why our identity must be continually revealed through our 'dying to ourselves' and being birthed out of His identity.

When I try and operate in human authority I fail every time. When I hide myself inside of Christ and walk in His authority, demons tremble, and hell shrinks back! Properly aligning my person the way God has set up the order to be has helped me tremendously. From my marriage to my home, family, and ministry, walking in God's authority and allowing His presence to discipline me, this discipline causes me to rejoice in who I am becoming rather than the human failure I experienced before.

Once I learned that this entire earth experience is not about me, but rather about Christ being revealed in me, my life became easier. My journey became a daily examination of who is in the lead of my life, heart, mind and thinking. When Christ leads I am assured, and confident within His presence. When I am leading I am unsure, and insecure, always needing assurances from those around me, exhausting them and frustrating them on a regular basis.

Are people continually frustrated with your constant need of approval and assurance? Be honest with yourself on this. Write down those areas where you frustrate yourself and others. These are the areas where you need to 'die to yourself' and allow the Lord to rule and reign within you.

_____
_____
_____
_____
_____
_____
_____
_____
_____

Through God's word we have been given His authority. Through our relationship with Christ and allowing Him to be Lord over our lives we have His authority.
Go through this checklist in your own life and see where you truly stand within the position of Christ's authority.

Authority is not about power; authority is about His presence.

Authority is not about who is in charge but about who is responsible.

Authority is not about who is on top and taking the credit but about who is willing to take the blame when necessary.

Authority is not about being #1, but rather about being submitted to #1!

Authority is not about commanding respect but about being respectful.

Authority is not about demanding anything but about submitting to the outcome of all things through Christ.

Authority is not about position, but about commission.

Authority is not about knowing what to say, but about knowing when not to say anything.

How did you measure up to His authority? God's authority is about disciplining yourself to always be about Him and never be about you! Lucifer was thrown to the earth and lost his worship position of authority because he would not discipline his heart to stay low. His heart became 'lifted up' and he lost his position. Once he was cast to the earth he stayed all about himself and did not change. We see this in the scripture in Luke 4:6-7.

"And the devil said to Him, 'All this authority I will give You, and their glory; for this has been delivered to me, and I give it to whomever I wish. Therefore, if You will worship before me, all will be Yours."

How completely deluded the devil was to think he had any authority at all. Jesus, the Son of God, has all authority. The devil was so self-deceived that he actually thought he had something to give to Jesus Christ, the Son of God! We would call him delusional and even pathological. It seems that the devil actually believed the lies he was telling Jesus, which would make him a pathological liar. He is deemed the author of lies so that would be a fitting description.

As you can see from this above scripture, the devil wanted the Son of God's worship! The devil actually said to Jesus, "If You will worship before me . . . "!

Jesus was being tempted, just like we are tempted, to worship something, anything other than almighty God. Jesus did not fall for this trick, but how many times do people who are called to worship God only, fall for this temptation? Many people who are created to be worshipers of the most high God fall simply by worshiping something else! We must discipline ourselves to not fall for this temptation. The first place we must look is within ourselves to make sure we are not worshiping ourselves! When worship becomes more about the music, the job, the gig, the show, the set, the sound, the lights, and the one who is singing, playing, dancing, etc,. we have already fallen and lost our position! Worship is all about the One being worshiped! It must never become about the worshipers. Never!!!

Do you need to stop and repent for a moment for the times you have personally made worship more about you, your sound, your monitor, your microphone, etc? Take a moment for self-examination and repentance. We all need to repent of this. We love the applause, the accolades, the acceptance, and the glory. But none of this belongs to us. It all belongs to Him. I repent of making worship about me, of those times when (you finish the sentence) . . .

_____

_____

_____

Discipline means 'making disciples'. We want to be disciples of Christ. We say we do at least, until it comes to giving up something, or dying to ourselves, or laying something down at His feet. We cringe when it means 'I' need to change instead of someone or something else that needs to change. When we get challenged to be different as a worshiper, what do we do? We start looking for an exit plan, somewhere else to go where 'I can be appreciated; where they understand me better; where the leadership truly understands what I am trying to accomplish here, etc.'

Instead of digging in and disciplining ourselves to be submitted and obedient to leadership we start looking for another home to go to where our gifts and talents can be appreciated. How undisciplined is that? It takes discipline to stay when it gets hard. It takes submitting to the authority of others to find out what the Lord truly wants of you.

I am not saying that there is never a time to leave and journey on to the next place. I am saying that you should make sure you are being led by the Spirit of God and not by your own uplifted heart and flesh. Make sure you are totally and completely disciplining your flesh to be under the authority of almighty God. This is the same God that actually allowed Joseph to be thrown into a pit, sold into slavery, thrown into prison, left and forgotten time and time again. This is the same God that allowed David to be hated by King Saul, hunted like an animal, as he hid in caves! This same God allowed David to be left out in the field when the prophet Samuel came to anoint the next king, and his own father did not even bother to bring him in from the field.

You may be disregarded by people, by your own family, or church, but maybe you have been set apart for a season of growth and discipline. You may be in a time where you are being prepared for what is coming in your life and ministry. Don't disregard your training. Don't allow the enemy to lie to you and cause you to have to circle this promise more than once to fully discipline yourself enough to learn the lesson here.

What places have you been set apart that at the time you felt you had been completely forgotten only to learn God had you on the back side of the desert disciplining and training you for things to come?

_____

_____

Do you want to be loved by the Lord? Proverbs 3:12 states, "Whom the Lord loves He corrects."

Proverbs 12:1, "Whoever loves instruction loves knowledge, but he who hates correction is stupid."

Are you one who loves correction, instruction and knowledge? If you can say yes to that then you are not stupid! Any other answer leads to the same 'stupid' place.

When we are walking in God's authority and in His discipline we will always be able to be used by the Lord.

II Kings 3:14-15, "And Elisha said, 'As the Lord of hosts lives, before whom I stand, surely were it not that I regard the presence of Jehoshaphat king of Judah, I would not look at you, nor see you. But now bring me a musician.' Then it happened, when the musician played, that the hand of the Lord came upon him."

This is a perfect example of people who are called by God working together to bring about God's desired results. Elisha was the prophet at this point in the story. He had taken Elijah's position and the king needed to hear from heaven. Elisha did not want to prophesy to the king but disciplined himself to do so regardless of how he felt at that moment in the natural. But he also realized then, as many of us realize now, that tones, music, and sounds can help us get into the realm of the prophetic much quicker when we discipline ourselves to be used by the Spirit of God. Elisha said to bring him a musician. This is supposition on my part but I would imagine Elisha had a particular musician he liked to work with, and maybe even a particular instrument that he flowed better with than others.

I grew up playing piano. That was and still is my instrument. When I am happy, sad, need to pray, need to repent, etc. I go to the piano or the keyboard. When I need to take the service to a particular place and feel the Lord leading me to do so, I find a keyboard or piano for my fingers! Then I can more quickly access the presence of God and with some practice and discipline, I can yield my spirit, my fingers, and my voice to be used for His glory.

What helps you get into the flow and presence of God? Is it a sound, an instrument, a cd, prayer, praying in tongues?

_____
_____
_____
_____
_____
_____
_____
_____
_____

Music is a powerful tool in the hands and heart of a disciplined worshiper. But without the deepest of relationships with our Creator, music can be used to bring about selfish motives and fulfill man's desires instead of God's will. We must guard against the temptation to use our gifts in services in our own strengths and abilities rather than being led by the Holy Spirit.

No one else may be able to tell when the Spirit of God is not leading us, but we know the difference. We know. Our own hearts condemn us when we are relying on our gifts and talents rather than being led of the Spirit. What are good ways to check yourself during a service?

_____

_____

What thoughts are going through your mind while you are worshiping on the platform?

_____

_____

Always check your own heart, thoughts, and ideas by Lucifer and his loss of position in Ezekiel 28:12-19, "You were the seal of perfection, full of wisdom and perfect in beauty.

You were in Eden, the garden of God; every precious stone was your covering: the sardius, topaz, and diamond, beryl, onyx, and jasper, sapphire, turquoise, and emerald with gold. The workmanship of your timbrels and pipes was prepared for you on the day you were created.

You were the anointed cherub who covers; I established you; you were on the holy mountain of God; you walked back and forth in the midst of fiery stones. You were perfect in your ways from the day you were created, till iniquity was found in you.

By the abundance of your trading you were filled with violence from within and you sinned; therefore I cast you as a profane thing out of the mountain of God; and I destroyed you, O covering cherub, from the midst of the fiery stones.

Your heart was lifted up because of your beauty; you corrupted your wisdom for the sake of your splendor; I cast you to the ground, I laid you before kings that they might gaze at you.

You defiled your sanctuaries by the multitude of your iniquities, by the iniquity of your trading; therefore I brought fire from your midst; it devoured you, and I turned you to ashes upon the earth in the sight of all who saw you.

All who knew you among the peoples are astonished at you; you have become a horror, and shall be no more forever."

This could hardly be any plainer, what happened to Lucifer as the lead worshiper. Pride got the best of him. Verse 17 in the Message Bible reads, "Your beauty went to your head. You corrupted wisdom by using it to get worldly fame."

Is this the most amazing statement? Doesn't this sound like what we all fight as worshipers in our society today? Our talents and gifts must not go to our heads and fill us with pride. Our wisdom must not be corrupted and used for worldly purposes and fame. What can you do to better to keep your own heart in check? What are some signs in your own life of when your pride is taking over?

_____

_____

_____

_____

Pride cost Lucifer his future in the kingdom of God. Do not go down the same road of prideful destruction and lose your God-given position within the kingdom! This can happen to anyone. If you are a worshiper it WILL HAPPEN TO YOU if you are not very careful to keep yourself submitted and disciplined at His feet on a daily basis.

In the very thought of, "This could never happen to me!" the sin of pride is ever present! This could and will happen to you, if you don't recognize the need to guard and protect your heart. This happened to Lucifer who started in the very presence of God. The only One who did not fall to this sin of pride is the only sinless and spotless One, Jesus Christ! We must hide ourselves within His presence if we have any hope of surviving and enduring until the end.

To whom much is given much is required (Luke 12:48) applies to those of us who have been given gifts and talents for His glory through worship. We have been given much but much is required of us. We must apply much discipline to keep ourselves pure and holy before Him.

Lord, help me to be more disciplined in:

_____
_____
_____
_____
_____
_____
_____
_____
_____
_____
_____
_____
_____

When we are wiling to lower ourselves to the lowest possible point at His feet, then and only then can we be used to our highest abilities through His highest authority. What else do you need to lay at His feet once and for all?

_____
_____
_____
_____
_____
_____
_____
_____

Chapter Thirteen
Being Worship

We are so driven by what we do, that most of our identities become about our 'doing' and we completely lose all identity in our 'being'. God's word is pointedly about our being, and not based upon our abilities to earn our way into His presence through what we do. If man could have done enough to be in God's presence, then the plan of salvation through Jesus Christ would have been unnecessary. But humanity could not earn its way; Jesus had to come and pay the price for us once and for all. As you look back over your life, in what ways have you tried to earn your way into a good enough position in your earth journey? Take a good look at yourself. Examine your childhood experience within your own family structure. What about your being accepted at school? What did you do to make sure you were one of the cool kids? What about as an adult? What traps can you quickly see as you take a good look over your daily routine of acceptance and approval?

_____
_____
_____
_____
_____

We are living in a day and a church age that doing worship has become totally acceptable, and not just acceptable but a requirement by most. Why and how has this slipped into our thinking? Doing worship is much easier than 'being' worship. Doing worship means I can practice enough, and make the sound good enough to get the people to engage, to get involved, to be moved, to get goose bumps! I can do worship at such a high level that the average person who comes to church and does not know the difference between the anointing of the Lord and a natural emotional feeling can be easily swayed into thinking, "Wow! Church was great today!" But if you ask them why church was so 'great' their responses would not be pleasing to the Lord most of the time.

Once again, please do not think that I am saying we should not practice, or be the best that we can be. Of course, practicing, learning the lyrics, and harmonies, and the parts are an absolute given! Of course, we should strive to be the best we can be within the realm of God's house. We study to show ourselves approved by the Spirit and purpose of God. We work hard to know more, do more, and be more of who we are called and created to be. But we cannot stop there. We must push even further than this if we are to finish strong as God's called and appointed worshipers!

Once we actually start dealing with our 'being worship' we will discover that 'doing worship' is easy compared to 'being worship'. Being worship requires my entire being, body, soul, and spirit to be engaged in the highest levels of 'dying to me' and being birthed by the Spirit of God.

We can teach music, playing and singing, dance and art. But we can't teach 'being'. God requires us to walk out our 'being' in all things. God's word requires us to:

Be saved.
Be holy.
Be filled with His Spirit.
Be righteous.
Be sanctified.
Be pure.
Be disciplined.
Be authoritative.
Be submissive.
Be worship.

It is in our being, not in our doing that we become acceptable as His highest worshipers in spirit and in truth. There is really no such thing, no such position as a worship leader. How can I lead you to worship? I can't lead you; I can only worship. You can follow me if you so choose, but my job is to worship the most high God. It is your responsibility as well.

We have allocated worship to a time frame within the beginning minutes of what we term a church service. But worship is not for a moment, or a season, or a service, or a time frame. Worship is a lifestyle, a way of living, a way of being. Worship is who I am, not something that I do. Worship is the intimate expression of my passion and hunger to know Him more, to be more intimately acquainted with Him. My soul longs for His presence and I am never satisfied with anything less than the fullness of His glory manifested.

No one can lead me to worship any more than I can lead someone else to worship. If this were true then worship would have a destination, which it does not. Worship is about heart, the heart that no man can see, or feel or even know. But God knows. He knows me deeply. He knows even those things and places that I hide from myself.

Worship is intimacy between humanity and Creator. Being worship is about my existence, pure and simple. My 'being worship' is for an audience of One, Creator, Orchestrator, Conductor, and Master.

Let's surrender ourselves, our beings, to the One who created us. Let's say this prayer of surrender together.

Let the words of my mouth and the meditation of my heart be acceptable in Your sight, my strength and my redeemer!
What can the instrument do apart from the One who is doing the playing? The instrument can do nothing apart from the One. So, here I am Lord, play me. Make me be Your melody, Your lyric, Your sound! Let me be the sound through which the world hears and recognizes the very existence of an all-powerful God! Let the world hear through me the sound waves of Your love, Your overpowering strength, Your pure and cleansing streams.

Lord, use me. Play me as Your instrument of pleasure. Let the sound waves of Your presence come forth beckoning, crying out, singing, renewing, reviving, quickening, all who long for You! Let them hear You through me. I have come before You, and I lay myself, this instrument at Your feet. Lord, come down from Your holy habitation, reaching down, and picking me up, into Your hands, Your mighty anointed hands; play the sounds of healing, and restoration. Play the sounds of Your glory, rising, cleansing all who will listen!

I am a woodwind instrument set before You to be played. Without the breath of Your divine presence, no sound of any value or worth can come forth. I am a stringed instrument laid at Your feet. Without Your divine fingers strumming, plucking, running over the reverberations of these yielded strings, no sound can come forth. I am any and all instruments awaiting the glorious and divine touch of Your presence. Without Your touch, I am a clanging cymbal and a sounding brass, a broken and unproductive sound wave that moves no one and goes nowhere.

Lord, I am Yours. I trust You. I will no longer belong to You part of the time, and myself part of the time. I belong to You. If there is no sound coming from me, then it is the divine Musician who wishes for this silence, not the instrument. This instrument no longer has a will, for I freely give my self, my will, my mind, my body, my instrument to my divine Creator.

May the light of Your glory be seen in me. May the sound of Your presence be heard through me. I am Yours and You are mine. This is My Beloved's song, an eternal love song, but only those who are washed clean by the blood of the Lamb can hear it.

Can you hear it? It is the sound of the redeemed crying loudly . . . even so,

"Come, Lord, Jesus!"

And the Bridegroom says, "I am coming quickly."

And the bride says, "Come, Lord, Jesus."

And the Bridegroom says, "I am coming soon."

And the bride says, "Come, Lord, Jesus."

And the Bridegroom says, "Behold! It is finished; I am coming."

And the bride says, "Even so! Come, Lord, Jesus!"

What would you like to say to your Bridegroom Jesus that is private between the two of you?

_____

_____

_____

_____

_____

_____

_____

_____

_____

_____

_____

_____

Chapter Fourteen
Restoration of Worship

In your own life where do you see that your worship could be restored? Where has it been broken? What places need restoration so you can be the worshiper God created you to be? Where have you been wounded that God could heal if you would trust Him to do so?

_____
_____
_____
_____
_____
_____
_____
_____

In II Kings 23 we find an amazing story of a king whose sole purpose was to restore worship, cleanse the altars of God and bring down those who had opposed God's purified worship. Open your Bible, or your We Who Worship book and read this chapter. You will find that King Josiah did all that he possibly could do in the natural to purify, clean up, and restore worship, but in all honesty, the only way to purify and clean up worship is to clean up worshipers. No one can do that for us. We must do it ourselves. I can clean myself up, you can clean yourself up, but you can't clean me up nor can I clean you up!

In this story the corruption had gone on for generations, and that is the way it is for most of us. Our diversion usually begins with one little thing, then another, then another until we are completely off track and in need of God's correction and ultimately His restoration. If we are not careful we can be just like the people in this story in II Kings. The sins of the forefathers had taken root in the hearts of the present generation. What can you see in this generation of worship that came as a result of an unresolved issue in a past generation? What about humanity's desire to have 'stars'? Heroes and superstars . . . even all the 'super heroes' we train our kids to look up to through all the cartoons, get us started on elevating someone other than the Lord God! We must be so careful to keep Jesus on the throne, and not put those with great voices, or amazing gifts of music, and talent on a pedestal and worship those people instead of the Lord.

Restoring worship was not about music, or singers, or dancers, or people. Restoring worship was about restoring God's altars and God's people in purification. God's altars have been broken down and we must open the altars in our sanctuaries up again and allow people to come and spend time with the Lord. People need time at the altar to personally be with the Lord, without the interference of well-meaning people who want to help. I'm not saying that we don't need others to help us pray. Sometimes we do, but then there are times when we need to learn to be 'alone with God' at the altar and not be worried what others might be thinking or saying.

Usually it comes down to my personal altar being purified and made ready. What do I have in my own life that hinders me from being restored? What am I holding on to, that I simply have not been able to give up and trust God with this particular thing, person, place, event, past experience, future hope?

_____
_____
_____
_____
_____
_____
_____

You are to keep yourself clean and purified by the Lord. You are to stay in His face, and in His fire. What others do is up to them. You can tell them, make it easier for them, but ultimately their own hearts, minds, and lives are set in motion by their own choices. This can be discouraging when you can so plainly see what others need to do, but it's not up to you to purify them or rebuild their personal altars. It's up to you to worship God. It's up to you to obey the Spirit of God. It is up to you to stay disciplined and submitted to His plan and purpose. The rest is up to them. It's a full-time job to keep myself pure, holy, and righteous before the Lord, and to keep my own altar rebuilt and restored in His presence.

As a worshiper you must fight against becoming discouraged. Discouragement can cost you your future. Discouragement can cause you to get so far off the track and plan of God that He will have to call someone else to finish what He has called you to do! This happened with Elijah, when he became so discouraged and disappointed because of Jezebel. Guard your own heart against the Jezebels of life. Protect your heart and keep yourself clean before Him.

God has entrusted us with the high calling and position of worshiper in His kingdom. Will we arise to this challenge or sink back into the self-focus of pride, arrogance, and self-image (whether lifted up, or poor image, all still rooted in pride of self), only to leave our most high and awesome God without His due worship?

We can call on the One in Isaiah 58:12-14 "And your ancient ruins shall be rebuilt; you shall raise up the foundations of [buildings that have laid waste for] many generations; and you shall be called Repairer of the Breach, Restorer of Streets to Dwell in. If you turn away your foot from [traveling unduly on] the Sabbath, from doing your own pleasure on My holy day, and call the Sabbath a [spiritual] delight, the holy day of the Lord honorable, and honor Him and it, not going your own way or seeking or finding your own pleasure or speaking with your own [idle] words, then will you delight yourself in the Lord, and I will make you to ride on the high places of the earth, and I will feed you with the heritage [promised for you] of Jacob your father; for the mouth of the Lord has spoken it."

Each one of us has ancient ruins of our internal worship that need to be restored. I cannot be used to help others repair and restore the altars of their hearts until I can allow the Lord who calls Himself 'Repairer of the Breach, Restorer of Streets to Dwell in' to repair and restore my own heart's altar. Can you trust Him to do this in your personal worship? What places of your heart can you give Him that need restoring, repairing, and rebuilding? He is the Lord. He will do what He will do, but we must trust Him to do it! Can you put into your own words the broken places that you have 'learned to live with'?   Can you put into your own words those areas you see as you pray and seek the Lord's face that He is requiring of you to give to Him? Won't you trust Him to rebuild you from the inside out? Tell Him in your own words what you need Him to rebuild.

_____
_____
_____
_____
_____
_____
_____
_____
_____
_____

Tell Him those areas, people, and situations that you desire His intervention and help in restoring.

_____
_____
_____
_____
_____
_____
_____
_____

Lord, rebuild and restore my . . .

_____
_____
_____
_____
_____

Take a moment to seek His face and ask Him to write a song of restoration through you right now. It may only be four lines, or two lines, or eight lines, or one line. It does not matter, for no one will hear it but the One who gave it to you. Write it out for Him.

_____
_____
_____
_____
_____
_____
_____
_____
_____
_____

Chapter Fifteen
Heaven and Earth Worship

God is requiring us as His worshipers to sing on two levels of worship. We can sing, and play, and dance, and do beautiful prepared worship unto our God. We can sing prepared songs that have been written and beautifully arranged, that many people know. We can sing lyrics and melodies that are very familiar from hymns, to spiritual songs, even singing the scriptures that we have memorized.

Then we are also required by the scriptures to sing a new song unto the Lord! These are songs of the Spirit of God that come forth from our very beings when we yield our entire personalities, talents, and gifts before His throne for Him to play us for His glory!

I have spent many hours before the Lord in meditation of eleven verses in the book of Revelation 4. Verse 9 starts out with, "And they sang a new song, saying . . ." They sang a new song! They sang a new song!

There are several references where singing a new song is a command from the Lord. Psalm 33:3, "Sing to Him a new song; Play skillfully with a shout of joy."

Psalm 96:1, "Sing to the Lord a new song! Sing to the Lord, all the earth!" (NET)

Revelation 5:9, "And they sang a new song, saying . . . " (ASV)

Singing a new song unto the Lord is a commandment. If we get tired of singing the same songs over and over can you imagine how the One who is totally creative gets tired of hearing the same songs over and over? And yet, when we study the sounds of heaven's worship, we hear and see the same phrases over and over, "Holy, Holy, Holy! Is the Lord God almighty! Who was and is and is to come!" "Worthy is the Lamb who was slain, to receive power and riches and wisdom, and strength and honor and glory and blessing!" "Blessing and honor and glory and power be to Him who sits on the throne, and to the Lamb, forever and ever!"

Certain phrases like these are used throughout all descriptions of heaven's worship songs! Saying who He is, is a prerequisite for heaven's worship. So I would think if we are to be able to call 'heaven to earth' through our worship then we write songs, whether by the Spirit in writing a new song, or by preparing a song, writing it down, charting it, and teaching it to a team of worshipers, we should consider writing melodies with lyrics that continually say back to God who He is, and what He does!

Take a moment to write Him a new song. Tell Him who He is to you. Tell Him what He has done for you. Just tell Him. He longs to hear you say it. He longs to hear you sing it! This is for His ears. Don't worry about it being good, or sounding great. Don't worry about the lyrics making sense to anyone because He gets you!

_____
_____
_____
_____

_____
_____
_____
_____
_____
_____
_____
_____

Don't compare your songs, or your sounds to anyone else. Just write. Sing. Play. Dance. Whatever it is He has gifted you to do, do it. Whatever it is He is telling you to do, do it. Better yet, 'be it'.

Lucifer was made with musical instruments within his being and he lost it all because he was lifted up in his heart instead of lifting God up with his worship! Don't get caught in thought! Don't get all caught up in your thought life and forget who is God is in all of this! He is God! You are a worshiper. Worship Him. Don't disqualify yourself before you even get started. You are covered with a garment of praise the Bible states in Isaiah 61:3. So wear it, and be it! You are covered by God with His coverings of praise. You don't cover yourself; He covers you with praise, so put on your garments of praise and take off your garments of heaviness. Wear His worship and praise! Sing! Verse 4 goes on to declare, "And they shall rebuild the ancient ruins; they shall raise up the former desolations and renew the ruined cities, the devastations of many generations."

Wearing your proper covering garments can help you rebuild and restore and raise up ruined cities and devastated generations! So sing, write songs, let Him play you for His glory. Sing in tongues, and put melodies to His sounds. Then ask Him to give you the interpretation and just sing it out in English. Don't say, "I don't have anything," just because you don't know what to say in English. You didn't know what to say in tongues either but you opened your mouth and He filled it! You interpret the same way. Pure and simple surrender and obedience will cause you to step into the interpretation just like it helped you to step into the singing and speaking in tongues in the first place! Yield yourself to the highest level and worship Him with a new song!

I know this is ever ongoing, an onslaught on your mind and heart to keep it real before the Father God. I know the battle you have to continually stay in with your own flesh, and soul. But this is a battle worth fighting because it has already been won for you through the cross of Christ. You must be crucified with Christ to be able to stand in these last days of worship unto our God.

Satan does not want you wearing your garments of praise and your robes of righteousness. He wants you to think that these coverings are not enough to cover our sins. But the fact is Jesus has already covered our sins, and washed our sins away by His blood coverings! Without the robes of righteousness and garments of praise we don't have what we need to show His glory! So put on your coverings and show forth His glory! Worship Him in spirit and in truth for His glory!

What else can you think of that you can personally do to continually keep yourself in position?

_____
_____
_____
_____
_____

How can you keep your robes of righteousness and your garments of praise in place as your covering of worship?

_____
_____
_____
_____
_____
_____

What are you being trained for through this earthly School Of Worship that can you can carry you from earth worship into heavenly, eternal worship?

_____
_____
_____
_____
_____
_____

Can you find a Psalm that you would like to write a melody for and sing to His throne? Use the music staff below to write the melody if you know music.

_____
_____
_____
_____
_____

_____
_____
_____
_____
_____

_____
_____
_____
_____
_____

Chapter Sixteen
Wordless Worship and Weeping Worship

There are many different kinds of worship that come to mind when I say wordless worship. I grew up in the Methodist church and wordless worship in my younger days could mean silent worship. But this is not what I am talking about in this case. I am talking about a worship so deep within you that no words can express the depths of your worship. Sometimes this is because of something that has happened to you, like someone has died and gone to heaven in front of you and you need to worship through your grief. No words will come out. But there is a type of worship that has no sounds, or words, but it's a heart-to-heart worship only you can give to the Lord.

There have been times in my life when worshiping the Lord was the only way I could survive the onslaught of the enemy. Going through the grief of our daughter dying, or having cancer, or our daughter-in-love, Stephanie, being diagnosed with a brain tumor, were times when worshiping the Lord without words was the most powerful tool I had to keep my victory. Sometimes in the darkest of hours we must worship, and yet our 'words' cannot be trusted to be strong, or faith, or even trust. Sometimes in these dark hours our words want to blame, or shame, or even worse, sound out despair! It's at these times that we can slip into wordless worship, sighs and groans that only the Spirit of God can interpret what we are truly saying!

II Corinthians 5:4, "For while we are still in this tent, we groan under the burden and sigh deeply (weighed down, depressed, oppressed) – not that we want to put off the body (the clothing of the spirit), but rather that we would be further clothed, so that what is mortal (our dying body) may be swallowed up by life [after the resurrection]. (Amplified Bible)

Our flesh has a voice and it wants to make sounds that are not beneficial many times in the midst of the battle. The scripture above calls our flesh, our tent. We should never allow our 'house' to have a voice. Our house is not who we are! And yet, when you stump your toe in the middle of the night, what flies out is not your spirit man but rather your 'tent' is crying out from pain.

Can you think of times when you now realize your flesh was talking, your tent was sounding off, and you need to repent of those words that were said? Even though it is not really who we are, we are responsible for our 'tent' (flesh), and we must repent when we do not keep it under and allow it to have a voice within us.

_____
_____
_____

We must build up our spirit to be stronger than our flesh. Whichever 'dog' you feed is the one that is in the lead, and is definitely the loudest. So when you fast and pray, starving your flesh, and bringing it under, you can pray more effectively because your spirit who is praying is now leading your flesh that is weak.

What are some areas in your personal life in which you know you need to starve your flesh, and feed your spirit? What are some areas where you still struggle with your flesh being in the lead? It may be food, or your mouth, or your attitude. It may be an actual 'sin' that you have allowed to stay hidden inside your heart. Maybe you have 'nursed' an old wound, a word spoken by someone, or an action that hurt you, scarred you deeply. What is it that you need to give to Him forever, and start 'forever' today?

_____

_____

_____

_____

II Timothy 1:6 tell us to "stir up the gift of God within us." The Spirit of God is most definitely the gift of God. We need to continually stir the Holy Spirit up within us after we have received Him and have the evidence through speaking and singing in tongues. When we don't rely on the Holy Spirit though and we continually strengthen our flesh instead of our Spirit, our flesh leads us instead of the Holy Spirit who is supposed to be leading us!

II Timothy 1:7 continued to expound upon this by adding, "For God has not given us a spirit of fear, but of power and of love and of a sound mind."

The fact is fear is the opposite of faith. Walking in fear is walking in the flesh. God did not give us that spirit, so the devil must have given it. When you accept fear as a part of your personality, or a part of your family and you dismiss this scripture by saying something like, 'My family has always had a lot of fear,' then you are bound to deal with it yourself. It is going to rule over you, and probably your children too, if you don't find the power of the Holy Spirit within you and allow Him to rise up!

God does not give me fear. God gives me power. God gives me love. God gives me a sound mind. When you look at the entire sentence, it is easy to see what the truth is here. The devil gives fear. God gives power. The devil gives fear. God gives love. The devil gives fear. God gives a sound mind. I would think that when you operate in fear, then you have no power, no love, and no sound mind. Looking at it that way, makes it very simple, what I must do. I must believe God for His Spirit to rise up inside me, and help me! I will not fear. I will not allow any fear anywhere near my dwelling. I will not allow fear in my life, my thinking, my mind, my house, or my family. Fear, you must go in Jesus' name!

Why have I taken this time to deal with fear? Many people, who are supposed to be walking in a higher level of worship, do not do so because of the spirit of fear. It has become a 'familiar, family' spirit because it has been with you so long that you are used to it. You may not like it but you are used to it so it stays, and you let it stay.

If you want to be the worshiper that God has called you to be, then stir up the gift of God, the Holy Spirit within you. Arise with His power, love and sound mind, and put fear out once and for all. Make sure the spirit of fear knows who you are in Christ.   Take authority over that evil, demonic thing and send it packing forever. In what areas have you allowed fear to be a resident inside of you?

_____
_____
_____
_____
_____

Psalm 6:6-10, "I am weary with my groaning; all night I soak my pillow with tears. I drench my couch with my weeping. My eye grows dim because of grief; it grows old because of all my enemies. Depart from me, all you workers of iniquity, for the Lord has heard the voice of my weeping. The Lord has heard my supplication; the Lord receives my prayer. Let all my enemies be ashamed and sorely troubled; let them turn back and be put to shame suddenly. (Amplified Bible)

Worship is prayer and intercessory prayer is worship.   They are one and the same.

Romans 8:23, "And not only the creation, but we ourselves too, who have and enjoy the first fruits of the [Holy] Spirit [a foretaste of the blissful things to come] groan inwardly as we wait for the redemption of our bodies [from sensuality and the grave, which will reveal] our adoption (our manifestation as God's sons.) (Amplified Bible)

Whether you are laughing or crying, whether you are loud or quiet, whether you are dancing or grieving make everything you do, and all that you are, be worship to your God and King! What else can you think of that you have never done before that you can turn into worship every day?

_____
_____
_____
_____

Pray and seek the Lord a moment or two, quietly right now, and ask Him what is another way is in corporate worship that you can show forth the glories of His presence. What have you never done (clap your hands, dance, sing loudly, move around, shout!) that you could start doing simply to bring your flesh under? Why would it bring your flesh under? Because if by this time you have never done it, you are probably embarrassed, as it may be completely out of your comfort zone. So here we are before His throne, and He is asking you to give Him what?

_____
_____
_____
_____

When the Spirit of the Lord comes upon a service there are times when He wants complete and holy silence. Are you able to give Him your silence as well as your sound? Have you spent enough time at His feet, just being with Him, that you can be completely comfortable with Him totally in control?   He is asking for silence at times. Can you give it to Him? Can you totally trust Him enough to be still, be silent, and listen carefully enough to know how to stay in the Spirit and move the service on to the next place without breaking the power of the moment?   Tell Him your thoughts on this new concept of worship.

_____
_____
_____
_____
_____
_____
_____

I'll give you a lesson in God worship.   That's an actual scripture! It's in the Message Bible in Psalm 34:9-11, "Worship God is you want the best; worship opens doors to all his goodness. Young lions on the prowl get hungry, but God-seekers are full of God. Come, children, listen closely; I'll give you a lesson in God worship."

I want God to give me a lesson in God worship. Do you? I want to know how to worship Him the way He deserves to be worshiped. Not from my puny, human, lower, slower nature, but higher, higher, higher until I am only with Him. When we have left our performances behind, our desires to please others, and move people, then we can step into God's kind of worship. It's a journey, one that will take you a lifetime to finish . . . even an eternal lifetime.   We will never reach the end of worship. Throughout eternity, we will fill heaven with our worship.

What is God saying to you right now? Ask Him to give you something higher than you have ever heard before, something higher than you have ever seen before. Ask Him to show you the depths of Him!   Ask Him!!! Write down what He says to you!

_____
_____
_____
_____
_____
_____
_____
_____
_____
_____
_____

I worship You, Lord, in spirit and in truth.
I worship You, Lord, in joy and in tears.
I worship You, Lord, in sounds and in silence.
I worship You, Lord, because You are my God and You deserve to be worshiped.

Chapter Seventeen
Prophetic Vision of Worship

Many times the Lord speaks to me through visions. In the two worship books I have written, We Who Worship and Rebuilding the Ruins of Worship, you will find visions throughout the texts. I closed the first worship book, We Who Worship, with a vision that I want to discuss with you. As you read the vision, I want you to consider what this means to you personally. What does this vision mean to our nation? Does this vision speak to me about my own life? What does this vision mean for our last days' generation of worshipers?

I was hovering over the curve of the earth in a desert place. There was a dead sea of sorts, mountains, hills, flat in between, dry, very dry. There was death everywhere but it was so intermingled amongst the people that they did not seem to notice the stench of death all over them. They were moving around, going about their daily routines, some were laughing at nothing, nonsense in the presence and purpose of Almighty God. Others were non-feeling, almost zombie-like in their motions, like the walking dead. Others were broken and crying, too weak to continue trying to make any sounds. I was being taken up higher so I could see from the beginning to the end. As I continued to pray by the Spirit of God, my eyes began to adjust to all I was seeing at once and I noticed something lying across the entire valley, across the desert floor. It was lying like a winding rope, snaking its way across the entire valley. Neither end of this 'thing' could be seen. It was as if it had neither a beginning nor an end. It was huge, beyond description in size. It lay like a Great Wall of China, miles and miles in the distance in both directions, lying as if dead, but not dead . . . only dormant. It was wide enough to walk upon, to ride upon in several vehicles at once. It was impenetrable, strong, and secure. It was immoveable, set in place as if it had taken possession of the land on which it lay.

My eyes adjusted even more and I noticed it had scales, like some sort of reptilian creature, but it looked petrified. No fluid, no water seemed present in its existence. It indeed looked completely dead, void of all life, huge but harmless just lying across the many miles of desert sand. People were all over it, climbing, driving, etc. with no fear or notice of it at all. It had been there so long, that humans had become accustomed to it being a part of their every day lives.

As I looked closer, fear began to grip my being and I began to whisper as I prayed to the Lord to show me what this was, lying so seemingly innocent across this dry, desert place. I whispered in prayer, "Lord, what is this? What am I seeing? What are You showing me?" The Lord quieted my spirit and told me, "Do not be afraid. Look closely."

As I peered at this thing I saw a slight shimmer, a movement beneath the moving feet of the unsuspecting and unprepared people. It only appeared to be lifeless. It was as if it slightly shook, almost like the big ole' ugly thing shivered. As I stared at this huge and still growing, horrible thing, I saw its scales just slightly opening up, and without even one person closest to it noticing, I saw eyes! It had eyes all over it, lots of ugly, yellow, devilish eyes showing itself as the predator it was, lying in wait for the unsuspecting to come even closer to it.

I wanted to scream to the people to get away from this hideous and insidious creature! I felt myself yelling to the people to wake up and look up! Notice what is right there beside you!!!! Yet, no matter how much I screamed and yelled, all the sounds coming forth from my being seemed to fall on deaf ears.

I frantically turned to the Lord who was looking on this scene unfolding before my eyes. I cried out to the Lord to help me sound the alarm! "Help me, Lord, to reach the people in time. Help me to help them!" He quickly and quietly touched me and said, "You obey Me. It will be what it will be."

What could this mean to you personally?

_____
_____
_____
_____

What could this mean to our worship in this generation?

_____
_____
_____
_____

What could this mean to our modern day church, as we know it?

_____
_____
_____
_____
_____

"It will be what it will be," says the Lord. What does that mean to you?

_____
_____
_____
_____

I am watching and listening, Lord. Use me. I am Your worship. Sing, play, dance, draw, do skits, make sound, or silence for Your glory, Lord. I am Your worship. It will be what it will be.

About the Author

Cheryl Salem walked the runway to become Miss America 1980, despite what appeared to be all odds stacked against her. A horrific car crash resulting in a physical handicap and over 100 stitches in her face, were no match for what God had planned for her life. Through childlike faith in Him, she overcame the obstacles and eventually took the crown in Atlantic City! She has used this distinction as a springboard to launch the Gospel into churches, conferences, and many television appearances. According to Cheryl, "None of these things would be possible, if not for my Jesus."

In 1985, Cheryl married the love of her life, Harry Salem II. Harry and Cheryl Salem travel the world ministering the gospel, telling people that Jesus loves them and that He is returning soon! Their lives revolve around seeking the Lord and where He would have them go. Two by two they travel, loving God's people, living and moving in His anointing.

In 1999, Harry and Cheryl endured the loss of their 6-year-old daughter, Gabrielle. As they boldly took steps of faith to overcome the agonizing pain of Gabrielle's death, they ask God to restore them and for souls to come into His kingdom. God has restored the Salem family and because of His mighty anointing, the altars have been full!

Harry and Cheryl are committed to leading godly lives as an example to others. Roman has married a beautiful young lady, Stephanie, and she has become their daughter-in-love. Healing and restoration has come full circle to the Salem family with the miracle birth of Roman and Stephanie's daughter, Mia Gabrielle and son, Roman Jr.

Harry Salem III continues in the family ministry as he has done since he was a child. He has completed his doctorate in Theology, while Roman and Stephanie are ministering as a couple to both youth and adult services across the country. Harry III, Roman and Stephanie minister with Harry and Cheryl in the Salem Family Ministries events.

Cheryl has recorded numerous music CDs, *I Am A Worshiper, Show Me your Glory* and the latest being *I AM Lullabies*. The most popular worship music she has released over the past few years are the four prophetic CDs of healing and restoration. Her prophetic flowing style on both the keyboard and vocally of the *Book of Revelation* and the *Book of Proverbs* are fast becoming the most requested music CDs! *I Am A Worshiper* and *I Am A Worshiper Workbook* are her latest books. She and her husband Harry have co-written 38 books with topics ranging from *Mourning to Morning* to *Entering Rest – Be Still.* Their book, *We Who Worship,* is designed to bring the reader into a deeper level of purity and intimacy with God in worship. Their marriage books *Two Becoming One* and *Don't Kill Each Other! Let God Do It!* are great books for couples to read and are also used for couples Bible studies together.

They love people and they love pouring themselves out because God's immense mercy, grace, and love keep them filled up in return.

The Spirit of God is flowing through Cheryl in an amazing way as He leads her to minister in a prophetic manner that involves a flow of music and teaching that is sung, instead of spoken. After surviving and overcoming cancer three times she believes that her call to rebuild and restore worship God's way is the mantle she will fulfill throughout the rest of her life.

Cheryl is a worshiper above all else. She ministers to ladies events across the country, encouraging women to reach their godly potential, but her main objective and central focus for Salem Family Ministries is to take Harry and Cheryl's unique, tag-team style of ministry into churches and gatherings all over this world, going out two by two, to reach families one by one for God's glory! (Luke 10:1-2)

Cheryl Salem

Books by Harry and Cheryl Salem

Tones of the Throne Room

Rebuilding the Ruins of Worship

Rebuilding the Ruins of Worship Workbook

We Who Worship

The Rise of an Orphan Generation: Longing for a Father

The Presence of Angels in Your Life

Don't Kill Each Other! Let God Do It!

Entering Rest – Be Still – A 40-Day Journey into the Presence of God

Obtaining Peace – A 40-Day Prayer Journal

2 Becoming 1

The Choice is Yours

Overcoming Fear – A 40-Day Prayer Journal

Every Body Needs Balance

From Grief to Glory

From Mourning to Morning

Distractions from Destiny

Speak the Word Over Your Family for Finances

Speak the Word Over Your Family for Healing

Speak the Word Over Your Family for Salvation

Fight in the Heavenlies*

It's Too Soon to Give Up*

Being #1 at Being #2

An Angel's Touch*

For Men Only

A Royal Child

The Mommy Book

How to Get a Balanced Body*

Simple Facts; Salvation, Healing & the Holy Ghost*

Health & Beauty Secrets*

Choose to be Happy*

Abuse ... Bruised but not Broken

You Are Somebody

A Bright Shining Place - The Story of a Miracle

*Check for availability

We would love to hear from you.   There are many ways to stay connected with us. You can receive our newsletter by giving us your email address through our web site. It's free and easy.

Salem Family Ministries
P. O. Box 1595
Cathedral City, CA 92234
www.salemfamilyministries.org

Like our page on Facebook
Salem Family Ministries

Subscribe to our YouTube channel
Salem Family Ministries

Connect through my Twitter account
Cheryl Salem @cherylsalem1980